LEON TROTSKY

WOMEN AND THE FAMILY

PATHFINDER PRESS, NEW YORK

Pathfinder Press, Inc.
410 West Street
New York, N.Y. 10014

Manufactured in the United States of America

CONTENTS

Introduction
  by Caroline Lund   7

From the Old Family to the New   19

A Letter to a Moscow Women Workers'
  Celebration and Rally   29

The Protection of Motherhood and
  the Struggle for Culture   31

To Build Socialism Means to
  Emancipate Women and Protect Mothers   45

Family Relations Under the Soviets   49

Thermidor in the Family   61

Notes   75

INTRODUCTION

By Caroline Lund

The Russian Revolution was begun by women. On International Women's Day in 1917 (March 8 in the Western calendar), women textile workers went out on strike in Petrograd and sent an appeal to other workers to support them. Their demands were modest — for bread, against the autocracy, and against the war — but this strike was the beginning of the revolution which was to culminate first in the overthrow of the czar and then in the overthrow of the capitalist class.

The living conditions of women, who were among the most downtrodden and oppressed in czarist Russia, were greatly improved by the revolution. The whole population has benefited from the industrialization made possible by the nationalization of industry and central planning. But, as Kate Millett points out in her book *Sexual Politics,* in only a short period after the Russian Revolution, the original progressive policies of the Soviet government toward the liberation of women were almost completely reversed. She writes:

> The initial radical freedoms in marriage, divorce, abortion, childcare, and the family were largely abridged and the reaction gained so that, by 1943, even coeducation was abolished in the Soviet Union. The sexual revolution was over, the counterrevolution triumphant. In the following decades conservative opinion elsewhere rejoiced in pointing to the Soviet as an object lesson in the folly of change. [*Sexual Politics,* Doubleday, New York, 1970, p. 176]

The fact that women have not achieved full liberation in the Soviet Union or in other countries which have had

socialist revolutions raises the obvious question: Is socialism the road to women's liberation? The basic demands
of the women's liberation movement certainly lead in the
direction of socialism, by spreading the idea that the functions of the family (child care, cooking, laundry, clean-
ing, medical care, etc.) should be socialized, that is, pro-
vided free for everyone. And yet, as Kate Millett notes,
in the Soviet Union many of the gains initially won
by women through the revolution were eventually lost.
The nuclear family system still exists and women are
still considered inferior persons, relegated to household
drudgery and child care and discriminated against in
employment.

Does the Soviet Union today represent the real possibilities under socialism? Is this all that is in store for
women under a new economic system? The writings of
Leon Trotsky collected in this pamphlet answer these
questions in the negative.

Trotsky, a central leader of the Bolshevik revolution,
was one of the greatest figures produced by the Marxist
movement. His views on women and the family are completely in the tradition of Frederick Engels's book *The
Origin of the Family, Private Property and the State.*
Trotsky's statement in *Problems of Life* (1924) — "In order to change the conditions of life, we must learn to
see them through the eyes of women" — is an excellent
expression of the Marxist tradition. After Lenin's death
in 1924, he was the chief opponent of the privileged bureaucracy headed by Stalin that usurped power in the
Soviet Union. Exiled in 1929, he maintained a revolutionary outlook up to his death in 1940, when Stalin's
agents finally succeeded in murdering him in Mexico.

The first two selections were written in 1923, when Lenin
was mortally ill, Trotsky was still commissar of war,
and the revolution was nearing the end of its first or
"heroic" phase. Conditions were very much in flux and
women were still making gains at the time. In these articles Trotsky grappled with the many complex material
and cultural problems faced by the Soviet Union in its
efforts to liberate women.

The third and fourth selections are from 1925, when

Trotsky had been removed from his military post, and the Left Opposition, which he headed inside the Communist Party, had begun to oppose the increasingly conservative policies promoted by the Stalin faction. Trotsky's speech and article were produced in connection with the Third All-Union Conference on the Protection of Mothers and Children, held in Moscow in December 1925.

The final selection is excerpted from Trotsky's book *The Revolution Betrayed,* written in Norway in 1936, when the Stalinist reaction had triumphed in all spheres of Soviet life. Here Trotsky analyzed the situation of women and the family as a part of the more general process of the degeneration of the revolution.

To put these articles by Trotsky in perspective, it is useful to look back over the changes in the situation of women in the Soviet Union.

Before 1917 women were in essence slaves of their husbands. The czarist law stated: "The wife is held to obey her husband, as the head of the family, to remain with him in love, respect, unlimited obedience, to do him every favor, and show him every affection, as a housewife." The czarist laws explicitly permitted a man to beat his wife. In some rural areas women had to wear veils and were not allowed to learn to read or write.

Between 1917 and 1927 the Soviet government passed a series of new laws giving women formal legal equality with men for the first time. The new laws made marriage an easy registration process which had to be based on mutual consent. Either partner could take the name of the other, or both could keep their own names. (For example, Trotsky took the name of his wife, Natalia Sedov, for citizenship requirements, and their sons also had her name.) The concept of illegitimate children was abolished. Free, legal abortion was made every woman's right. By 1927 a marriage did not even have to be registered, and divorce was easily possible on the request of one partner, with or without the knowledge of the other.

The 1919 program of the Communist Party stated:

> The party's task at the present moment is primarily work in the realm of ideas and education so as to

destroy utterly all traces of the former inequality or
prejudices, particularly among backward strata of
the proletariat and peasantry. Not confining itself
to formal equality of women, the party strives to
liberate them from the material burdens of obsolete
household work by replacing it by communal houses,
public eating places, central laundries, nurseries, etc.

The first steps toward bringing women out of the homes
and into the life of the country, as well as the overall effect of the revolution in undermining all backward traditions, had a great impact on the family. The family
system was shaken to its roots, and all kinds of experiments were tried out in new forms of communal living,
especially by young people.

But the program of the Bolsheviks was not fully realized, and during the 1930's a complete reversal occurred
in the Soviet attitude toward women and the family. The
perspective became one of maintaining the family rather
than replacing it, and many of the gains made by women
in the first ten years of the revolution were eliminated.
Abortions were made illegal and divorce was made more
and more difficult until it became an expensive court
procedure. Prostitutes were arrested, whereas the early
Bolshevik policy had been to arrest only the brothel own-
ers and expose the men who bought prostitutes and to provide voluntary job training for the prostitutes. The hours
of day-care centers were cut down to coincide with the
hours of the working day. And female children were taught
special subjects in the schools to prepare them for their
role as mothers and housewives.

Here is how Trotsky in 1938 summarized this process of reversal:

The position of *woman* is the most graphic and tell-
ing indicator for evaluating a social regime and state
policy. The October Revolution inscribed on its
banner the emancipation of womankind and created
the most progressive legislation in history on marriage and the family. This does not mean, of course,
that a 'happy life' was immediately in store for the

Soviet woman. Genuine emancipation of women is inconceivable without a general rise of economy and culture, without the destruction of the petty-bourgeois economic family unit, without the introduction of socialized food preparation, and education. Meanwhile, guided by its conservative instinct, the bureaucracy has taken alarm at the 'disintegration' of the family. It began singing panegyrics to the family supper and the family laundry, that is, the household slavery of woman. To cap it all, the bureaucracy has restored criminal punishment for abortions, officially returning women to the status of pack animals. In complete contradiction with the ABC of Communism, the ruling caste has thus restored the most reactionary and benighted nucleus of the class system, i.e., the petty-bourgeois family. [From *Writings of Leon Trotsky (1937-38),* Pathfinder Press, New York, 1970, p. 170]

After Stalin's death in 1953 some changes were made, such as restoring legalized abortions, but the basic perspective of maintaining the family as an economic unit has remained to the present day. An article in the February 1969 issue of *Soviet Life* about the new law on marriage and the family adopted by the Supreme Soviet in 1968 states: "As previously, the new Fundamental Law says that only a marriage which has been officially registered has legal force. This definition is vital to the central goal of Soviet family legislation, that is, to strengthen the family unit."

Soviet women today are still responsible for the full burden of housework and child rearing. A large percentage of preschool children are unable to attend nurseries and kindergartens.[1] Appliances such as refrigerators are still a luxury, and there is no wide-scale system of public laundries; laundry must be washed and hung up to dry in each tiny, overcrowded apartment.

Fifty percent of the wage earners in the Soviet Union are women, but they generally work at lower-paying jobs and are not proportionately represented in supervisory positions. For instance, women are 32 percent of all engineers but only 12 percent of plant directors; they are 73 percent of primary and secondary schoolteachers but only 23 percent of school directors; they are 42 percent of scientists but only two of the 204 members of the Soviet Academy of Scientists are women. Women are 79 percent of the doctors in the Soviet Union, but doctors receive only two-thirds the wage of a skilled worker, so men tend not to want to be doctors. In the political arena, only three of the 195 members of the Communist Party Central Committee are women.

The return to the bourgeois concept of the family and of women's "duties" within the family did not occur in isolation from other developments in the Soviet Union. It was part of a process which affected all spheres of Soviet life. A growth of privilege occurred; all democracy was abolished; a conservative foreign policy was adopted, based on "socialism in one country" instead of world revolution; the popular militia was abolished in favor of a standing army with a privileged officer caste; the arts were stifled; a piecework system of wage payments was instituted; oppression of national minorities was resumed; the young generation was repressed; purges eliminated the entire generation of Bolsheviks who made the revolution in 1917.

What occurred could be called a "backlash"—a political counterrevolution, a rolling back of the revolution, not to the point where capitalism was restored, but to where many vestiges of capitalist society were revived or fortified.

The basic reason for the triumph of the counterrevolution was the economic and political isolation of the revolution and the poverty of Soviet society. In addition to its extreme economic backwardness, Russia was devastated by World War I. Then the best, most conscious defenders of the revolution were killed in the civil war of 1918-21, during which Russia was invaded by twenty-one capitalist countries trying to crush the revolution. Some areas of the Soviet Union were reduced to a state of extreme famine during 1919 and 1921, even to the point where cannibalism sometimes occurred. The revolution was isolated for many years, without inspiration or aid from revolutions in any richer country.

Here is how Trotsky described the tendency toward the rise of the bureaucracy because of poverty:

> When there is enough goods in a store, the purchasers can come whenever they want to. When there is little goods, the purchasers are compelled to stand in line. When the lines are very long, it is necessary to appoint a policeman to keep order. Such is the starting point of the power of the Soviet bureaucracy. [*The Revolution Betrayed*, Pathfinder Press, New York, 1970, p. 112]

This layer of "policemen" and administrators who oversaw the distribution of the scarce goods grew rapidly. And, of course, they did not fail to siphon off the best goods for themselves. Thus, the privileged bureaucracy arose, with interests separate from those of the Soviet people. And the opposition to this growth of privilege was weakened because of the exhaustion of the revolution through wars and through its isolation as the only workers' state in a surrounding capitalist world.

In relation to the liberation of women, the extreme poverty inherited by the Russian Revolution meant two things: first, it meant objective limitations on how fast the Soviet government could move toward constructing alternatives to the family system (child-care centers, laundries, restaurants, etc.); and second, it contributed to the rise of the bureaucracy, which, as Kate Millett wrote, "stood Marxism on its head." The bureaucracy glorified the family as a "socialist" institution and used the repressive, authoritarian nature of the family as a prop to its own rule.

In the selections in this pamphlet, Trotsky's stress on the need for the development of culture and the elevation of the human personality stemmed from this economic and cultural backwardness. His references to the tragedy of broken homes, to the problem of alcoholism in poisoning human relations, and to the large numbers of homeless children and prostitutes all point to the brutalization of people by economic want. Superstitious, tra-

ditionalist attitudes were prevalent among women because
they were among the most oppressed. When child-care
centers were established, for instance, many women in
the countryside and even in the cities were distrustful
at first and hostile toward them.

This extreme backwardness and the lack of a well-
developed women's liberation movement are reflected in
Trotsky's frequent use of the terms "mother" and "wife"
as synonymous with "woman," in his lumping together
women and children, and in his call for "the protection
of motherhood." Part of the reason for this was that wom-
en and children shared an almost total economic dependence upon the father.

In all these writings, Trotsky emphasizes the fact that
a socialist revolution is only *one* necessary precondition
for the liberation of women. Another factor is the level
of material wealth and technological development of the
society. This was the crux of the problem in the Soviet
Union. The Russian Revolution was not simply a revolution against capitalism; it was also a revolution against
feudalism and czarism. It had to begin by catching up
to the advanced capitalist countries — by instituting land
reform and building up industry. Before this was accomplished, there was no basis for socialist relations between people, such as "to each according to his needs,"
or communal living arrangements.

Socialist revolutions have occurred so far only in eco-
nomically backward countries. This is the fundamental
reason why there are no countries to serve as models
for the liberation of women through a socialist revolution. A socialist revolution does not automatically produce socialism; it only creates conditions that make it
possible to build socialism. Trotsky characterized the Soviet Union as "a *preparatory* regime *transitional* from
capitalism to socialism." In some respects — and certainly
in regard to women — the Soviet Union is still closer to
capitalism than socialism, even now, when it has under-
gone substantial industrialization.

Kate Millett, in *Sexual Politics,* tries to grapple with
the problem of why the bureaucracy triumphed in the

Soviet Union. She correctly points out that women in the Soviet Union are far from being liberated and that their position is still basically the same as women in capitalist countries.

But her analysis is inadequate because she tries to evaluate the counterrevolution in the family in isolation from the general political counterrevolution which affected every area of Soviet life. She concludes that the major reason for the counterrevolution in family life and in the status of women was that "Marxist theory had failed to supply a sufficient ideological base for a sexual revolution, and was remarkably naive as to the historical and psychological strength of patriarchy" (p. 169). Later she writes: "In addition to this, there was no realization that while every practical effort should be made to implement a sexual revolution, the real test would be in changing attitudes" (p. 170). She notes that Trotsky vehemently denounced the regression to the patriarchal family in *The Revolution Betrayed,* but, she says, "this is the hindsight of 1936" (p. 170).

While it would have helped if the leaders of the revolution had had a deeper understanding of the process of the sexual revolution, it is way out of balance to see this deficiency as a major reason for the triumph of the bureaucracy. The highest level of consciousness in this area could not have prevented the triumph of Stalinism, which was based on the material factors of the poverty and isolation of the revolution.

No matter how much the leadership of the revolution might have attempted to fight the backward attitudes inherited from the patriarchal family traditions, no permanent progress could have been realized for the Soviet woman until steps were taken to *replace* the private household that imprisoned her and to end her dependence upon her husband. The fundamental need was to change the *institutions* that, in the final analysis, influence and determine attitudes. The Bolshevik program of Lenin and Trotsky's time was correct: to liberate women from their role as domestic slaves by replacing the private family household with communal forms of living.

Unfortunately, the real resources of the Soviet Union were insufficient to speedily implement the program of the Bolsheviks.

That Trotsky was also very much concerned with changing backward attitudes about women and the family can be seen in all the selections in this pamphlet; and that he recognized the special role of women organized to change both attitudes and practices is especially clear in his 1925 speech where he stresses the need for women to be the "moral battering ram" in changing the old relations.

Millett's remark about Trotsky's "hindsight of 1936" is also off the target. Trotsky was an opponent of the Stalinist "backlash" from 1923 on, that is, from its first appearance, and he gave the rest of his life, including his life itself, to implacable struggle against the entrenchment of Stalinism in every area of Soviet activity and in the international working-class movement. As early as 1927, in *The Platform of the Left Opposition,* Trotsky was demanding of the Soviet government, "We must restore to the workers the 'trifles' which have been taken away from them (day nurseries, tram tickets, longer holidays, etc.)."

The victory of the Stalinist bureaucracy, he warned — and he said this more than a decade before 1936 — would endanger *all* the social conquests of the revolution and revive the worst features of prerevolutionary Russia. Trotsky did not exclude the conditions of women in this farsighted prediction.

If Millett's remark is intended to imply that Trotsky should have been making the 1936 criticisms earlier, then it is a case of unhistorical reasoning. The political counterrevolution was a *process,* which consolidated itself only in the 1930s. It would have been wrong to assume, in the 1920s, that the degeneration of the revolution was a foregone conclusion. At any point along the way, a successful revolution in another country would have strengthened the revolutionary forces inside the Soviet Union and possibly prevented the consolidation of the Stalinist victory.

What is needed today is a continuation of the revolution of 1917, to carry it through to completion. It will require a political revolution to overthrow the present conservative, privileged bureaucratic leadership that now exists in the Soviet Union, and to move toward the elimination of privilege, the restoration of workers' democracy and a revolutionary perspective in all areas, including the liberation of women and replacement of the family.

The beginnings of this process can already be seen in the East Berlin uprising of 1953, the Hungarian Revolution of 1956, and the "Czech spring" in 1968. In the Soviet Union itself there is a proliferating underground of dissent and rebellion, which has been most visible through the works of dissident writers. A criticism of the reactionary policy of the bureaucracy toward the family is raised in the works of some of these writers, for example, in Solzhenitsyn's *The First Circle*. In this novel he writes:

Dasha was beginning her thesis for the third time. Her first subject had been 'Problems of Food Distribution under Socialism.' This subject had been very clear twenty years before, when every Pioneer, Dasha among them, would have known by heart that the family kitchen was a thing of the past and that liberated women would get their breakfasts and lunches in collective dining rooms. But over the years the subject had become clouded and even dangerous. Certainly whoever ate in a collective dining room — Dasha herself, for instance — did so only out of bleak necessity.

Only two forms of collective dining were prospering: the expensive restaurants — where the expression of the socialist principle was not all it might have been — and the cheapest little bars, selling only vodka. In theory, there were still the collective dining rooms, because the Great Coryphaeus [Stalin] had been too busy for the last twenty years to speak out on the subject of food distribution. So it was dangerous to risk speaking out on one's own. [p. 323]

The movements toward revolt and opposition in the
Soviet Union represent the interests of Soviet women.
Women, like Larissa Daniel who participated in a dem-
onstration in Moscow's Red Square against the Soviet
invasion of Czechoslovakia, are prominent among the
dissenters today, just as their forebears were prominent
in making the 1917 revolution.

It is inconceivable, with women's liberation movements
spreading throughout the world, that such a movement
will not appear in the Soviet Union too, or that it will
not play a leading role in the political revolution being
generated there now. One great lesson to be learned from
the Soviet experiences, both positive and negative, is the
need for women to organize as women *before* the socialist revolution and during the socialist revolution, so
that they will be able to play the maximum role (the
"battering ram" factor, to use Trotsky's terminology) inside the revolution to insure that their needs and aspirations are satisfied and not subordinated. This is a lesson
that applies to every country in the world — not only
the countries where the socialist revolution must be revived or rid of deformations but also countries like our
own, where the socialist revolution has yet to begin.

October 15, 1970

The second edition includes a magazine article that
Trotsky wrote in 1932, in response to some questions
put to him by the magazine, at a time when proposals
for United States recognition of the Soviet Union were
provoking considerable discussion of Soviet life.

FROM THE OLD FAMILY TO THE NEW

This article was printed in Pravda, *July 13, 1923. The first English translation, by Z. Vengerova, appeared in* Problems of Life *in 1924.*

The inner relations and happenings within the family are, by their very nature, the most difficult to investigate, the least subject to statistics. It is not easy, therefore, to say how far family ties are more easily and frequently broken nowadays (in actual life, not merely on paper) than formerly. To a great extent we must be content to judge by eye. The difference, moreover, between prerevolutionary times and the present day is that formerly all the troubles and dramatic conflicts in the working-class families used to pass unnoticed by the workers themselves; whereas now a large upper part of the workers occupy responsible posts, their life is much more in the limelight, and every domestic tragedy in their life becomes a subject of much comment and sometimes of idle gossip.

Subject to this serious reservation, there is no denying, however, that family relations, those of the proletarian class included, are shattered. This was stated as a firmly established fact at the conference of Moscow party propagandists,[2] and no one contested it. They were only differently impressed by it — each in his own way. Some viewed it with great misgivings, others with reserve, and still others seemed perplexed. It was, anyhow, clear to all that some great process was going on, very chaotically assuming alternately morbid or revolting, ridiculous or tragic forms, and which had not yet had time to disclose its hidden possibilities of inaugurating a new and higher order of family life.

Some information about the disintegration of the family

has crept into the press, but just occasionally, and in very vague, general terms. In an article on the subject, I had read that the disintegration of the family in the working class was represented as a case of "bourgeois influence on the proletariat."

It is not so simple as this. The root of the question lies deeper and is more complicated. The influence of the bourgeois past and the bourgeois present is there, but the main process consists in a painful evolution of the proletarian family itself, an evolution leading up to a crisis, and we are witnessing now the first chaotic stages of the process.

The deeply destructive influence of the war on the family is well known. To begin with, war dissolves the family automatically, separating people for a long time or bringing people together by chance. This influence of the war was continued and strengthened by the revolution. The years of the war shattered all that had stood only by the inertia of historic tradition. They shattered the power of czardom, class privileges, the old traditional family. The revolution began by building up the new state and has achieved thereby its simplest and most urgent aim.

The economic part of its problem proved much more complicated. The war shook the old economic order; the revolution overthrew it. Now we are constructing a new economic state — doing it as yet mostly from the old elements, reorganizing them in new ways. In the domain of economics we have but recently emerged from the destructive period and begun to ascend. Our progress is still very slow, and the achievement of new socialistic forms of economic life are still very distant. But we are definitely out of the period of destruction and ruin. The lowest point was reached in the years 1920-21.

The first destructive period is still far from being over in the life of the family. The disintegrating process is still in full swing. We must bear that in mind. Family and domestic life are still passing, so to speak, their 1920-21 period and have not reached the 1923 standard. Domestic life is more conservative than economic, and one of the reasons is that it is still less conscious than the latter.

In politics and economics the working class acts as

a whole and pushes on to the front rank its vanguard, the Communist Party, accomplishing through its medium the historic aims of the proletariat. In domestic life the working class is split into cells constituted by families. The change of political regime, the change even of the economic order of the state—the passing of the factories and mills into the hands of the workers—all this has certainly had some influence on family conditions, but only indirectly and externally, and without touching on the forms of domestic traditions inherited from the past.

A radical reform of the family and, more generally, of the whole order of domestic life requires a great conscious effort on the part of the whole mass of the working class, and presumes the existence in the class itself of a powerful molecular force of inner desire for culture and progress. A deep-going plow is needed to turn up heavy clods of soil. To institute the political equality of men and women in the Soviet state was one problem and the simplest. A much more difficult one was the next— that of instituting the industrial equality of women and men in the factories, the mills, and the trade unions and of doing it in such a way that the men should not put the women to disadvantage. But to achieve the actual equality of man and woman within the family is an infinitely more arduous problem. All our domestic habits must be revolutionized before that can happen. And yet it is quite obvious that unless there is actual equality of husband and wife in the family, in a normal sense as well as in the conditions of life, we cannot speak seriously of their equality in social work or even in politics. As long as woman is chained to her housework, the care of the family, the cooking and sewing, all her chances of participation in social and political life are cut down in the extreme.

The easiest problem was that of assuming power. Yet just that problem alone absorbed all our forces in the early period of the revolution. It demanded endless sacrifices. The civil war necessitated measures of the utmost severity. Philistine vulgarians cried out about the barbarization of morality, about the proletariat becoming bloody and depraved, and so on. What was actually

happening was that the proletariat, using the means of
revolutionary violence forced into its hands, was con-
ducting a struggle for a new culture, for genuine human
values.

In the first four or five years we have passed econom-
ically through a period of terrific breakdown. The productivity of labor collapsed, and the products were of
an appallingly low quality. Enemies saw, or chose to
see, in such a situation a sign of the rottenness of the
Soviet regime. In reality, however, it was but the inevitable
stage of the destruction of the old economic forms and of
the first unaided attempts at the creation of new ones.

In regard to family relations and forms of individual
life in general, there must also be an inevitable period
of disintegration of things as they were, of the traditions,
inherited from the past, which had not passed under the
control of thought. But in this domain of domestic life
the period of criticism and destruction begins later, lasts
very long, and assumes morbid and painful forms, which,
however, are complex and not always perceptible to super-
ficial observation. These progressive landmarks of critical
change in state conditions, in economics and life in general, ought to be very clearly defined to prevent our get-
ting alarmed by the phenomena we observed. We must
learn to judge them in their right light, to understand
their proper place in the development of the working
class, and consciously to direct the new conditions towards
socialist forms of life.

The warning is a necessary one, as we already hear
voices expressing alarm. At the conference of Moscow
party propagandists some comrades spoke with great
and natural anxiety of the ease with which old family
ties are broken for the sake of new ones as fleeting as
the old. The victims in all cases are the mother and children. On the other hand, who in our midst has not heard
in private conversations complaints, not to say lamen-
tations, about the "collapse" of morality among Soviet
youth, in particular among Komsomols?[3] Not everything
in these complaints is exaggeration — there is also truth
in them. We certainly must and will fight the dark sides
of this truth — this being a fight for higher culture and the

ascent of human personality. But in order to begin our work, to tackle the ABC of the problem without reactionary moralizing or sentimental downheartedness, we must first make sure of the facts and begin to see clearly what is actually happening.

Gigantic events, as we said above, have descended on the family in its old shape, the war and the revolution. And following them came creeping slowly the underground mole — critical thought, the conscious study and evaluation of family relations and the forms of life. It was the mechanical force of great events combined with the critical force of the awakened mind that generated the destructive period in family relations that we are witnessing now. The Russian worker must now, after the conquest of power, make his first conscious steps towards culture in many departments of his life. Under the impulse of great collisions, his personality shakes off for the first time all traditional forms of life, all domestic habits, Church practices, and relationships.

No wonder that, in the beginning, the protest of the individual, his revolt against the traditional past, is assuming anarchic, or to put it more crudely, dissolute forms. We have witnessed it in politics, in military affairs, in economics; here anarchic individualism took on every form of extremism, partisanship, public-meeting rhetoric. And no wonder also that this process reacts in the most intimate and hence most painful way on family relationships. There the awakened personality, wanting to reorganize in a new way, removed from the old beaten tracks, resorts to "dissipation," "wickedness," and all the sins denounced in the Moscow conference.

The husband, torn away from his usual surroundings by mobilization, changed into a revolutionary citizen at the civic front. A momentous change. His outlook is wider, his spiritual aspirations higher and of a more complicated order. He is a different man. And then he returns to find everything there practically unchanged. The old harmony and understanding with the people at home in family relationship is gone. No new understanding arises. The mutual wondering changes into mutual discontent, then into ill will. The family is broken up.

The husband is a Communist. He lives an active life, is engaged in social work, his mind grows, his personal life is absorbed by his work. But his wife is also a Communist. She wants to join in social work, attend public meetings, work in the Soviet or the union. Home life becomes practically nonexistent before they are aware of it, or the missing of home atmosphere results in continual collisions. Husband and wife disagree. The family is broken up.

The husband is a Communist, the wife is nonparty. The husband is absorbed by his work; the wife, as before, only looks after her home. Relations are "peaceful," based, in fact, on customary estrangement. But the husband's committee—the Communist "cell"—decrees that he should take away the icons hanging in his house. He is quite willing to obey, finding it but natural. For his wife it is a catastrophe. Just such a small occurrence exposes the abyss that separates the minds of husband and wife. Relations are spoiled. The family is broken up.

An old family. Ten to fifteen years of common life. The husband is a good worker, devoted to his family; the wife lives also for her home, giving it all her energy. But just by chance she comes in touch with a Communist women's organization. A new world opens before her eyes. Her energy finds a new and wider object. The family is neglected. The husband is irritated. The wife is hurt in her newly awakened civic consciousness. The family is broken up.

Examples of such domestic tragedies, all leading to the one end—the breaking up of the family—could be multiplied endlessly. We have indicated the most typical cases. In all our examples the tragedy is due to a collision between Communist and nonparty elements. But the breaking up of the family, that is to say, of the old-type family, is not confined to just the top of the class as the one most exposed to the influence of new conditions. The disintegrating movement in family relationships penetrates deeper. The Communist vanguard merely passes sooner and more violently through what is inevitable for the class as a whole. The censorious attitude towards old conditions, the new claims upon the family, extend far beyond the border line between the Communist and the working class as a whole.

The institution of civil marriage was already a heavy blow to the traditional consecrated family which lived a great deal for appearances. The less personal attachment there was in the old marriage ties, the greater was the binding power of the external forces, social traditions, and more particularly religious rites. The blow to the power of the Church was also a blow to the family. Rites, deprived of binding significance and of state recognition, still remain in use through inertia, serving as one of the props to the tottering family. But when there is no inner bond within the family, when nothing but inertia keeps the family itself from complete collapse, then every push from outside is likely to shatter it to pieces, while, at the same time, it is a blow at the adherence to Church rites. And pushes from the outside are infintely more likely to come now than ever before. That is the reason why the family totters and fails to recover and then tumbles again. Life sits in judgment on its conditions and does it by the cruel and painful condemnation of the family. History fells the old wood — and the chips fly in the wind.

But is life evolving any elements of a new type of family? Undoubtedly. We must only conceive clearly the nature of these elements and the process of their formation. As in other cases, we must separate the physical conditions from the psychological, the general from the individual. Psychologically the evolution of the new family, of new human relationships in general, for us means the advancement in culture of the working class, the development of the individual, a raising of the standard of his requirements and inner discipline. From this aspect, the revolution in itself has meant, of course, a big step forward, and the worst phenomena of the disintegrating family signify merely an expression, painful in form, of the awakening of the class and of the individual within the class. All our work relating to culture, the work we are doing and the work we ought to be doing, becomes, from this viewpoint, a preparation for new relationships and a new family. Without a raising of the standard of culture of the individual working man and woman, there cannot be a new, higher type of family, for in this domain we can only, of course, speak of inner discipline and not of external compulsion. The force then of the inner discipline of the individual in the family is conditioned by the tenor of the inner life, the scope and value of the ties that unite husband and wife.

The physical preparations for the conditions of the new life and the new family, again, cannot fundamentally be separated from the general work of socialist construction. The workers' state must become wealthier in order that it may be possible seriously to tackle the public education of children and the releasing of the family from the burden of the kitchen and laundry. Socialization of family housekeeping and public education of children are unthinkable without a marked improvement in our economics as a whole. We need more socialist economic forms. Only under such conditions can we free the family from the functions and cares that now oppress and disintegrate it. Washing must be done by a public laundry, catering by a public restaurant, sewing by a public workshop. Children must be educated by good public teachers who have a real vocation for the work. Then the bond between husband and wife would be freed from everything external and accidental, and the one would cease to absorb the life of the other. Genuine equality would at last be established. The bond will depend on mutual attachment. And on that account particularly, it will acquire inner stability, not the same, of course, for everyone, but compulsory for no one.

Thus, the way to the new family is twofold: (*a*) the raising of the standard of culture and education of the working class and the individuals composing the class; (*b*) an improvement in the material conditions of the class organized by the state. The two processes are intimately connected with one another.

The above statements do not, of course, imply that at a given moment in material betterment the family of the future will instantly step into its rights. No. A certain advance towards the new family is possible even now. It is true that the state cannot as yet undertake

either the education of children or the establishment of
public kitchens that would be an improvement on the
family kitchen, or the establishment of public laundries
where the clothes would not be torn or stolen. But this
does not mean that the more enterprising and progressive families cannot group themselves even now into collective housekeeping units. Experiments of this kind must,
of course, be made carefully; the technical equipment of
the collective unit must answer to the interests and requirements of the group itself, and should give mani-
fest advantages to every one of its members, even though
they be modest at first.

"This task," Comrade Semashko[4] recently wrote of the
necessity of reconstructing our family life,

> is best performed practically; decrees and moralizing
> alone will have little effect. But an example, an il-
> lustration of a new form, will do more than a thou-
> sand excellent pamphlets. This practical propaganda
> is best conducted by the method surgeons in their
> practice call transplantation. When a big surface is
> bare of skin either as the result of wound or burn,
> and there is no hope that the skin will grow suffi-
> ciently to cover it, pieces of skin are cut off from
> healthy places of the body and attached in islets on
> the bare surface; these islets adhere and grow until
> the whole surface is covered with skin.
>
> The same thing happens in practical propaganda.
> When one factory or works adopts Communist forms,
> other factories will follow. [N. Semashko, "The Dead
> Holds on to the Living," *Izvestia,* no. 81, April 14,
> 1923]

The experience of such collective family housekeeping
units, representing the first, still very incomplete approx-
imations to a Communist way of life, should be carefully
studied and given attentive thought. The combination
of private initiative with support by the state power —
above all, by the local Soviets and economic bodies —
should have priority. The building of new houses — and,
after all, we are going to build houses! — must be reg-

ulated by the requirements of the family group communities. The first apparent and indisputable success in this direction, however slight and limited in extent, will inevitably arouse a desire in more widespread groups to organize their life on similar lines. For a thought-out scheme, initiated from above, the time is not yet ripe, either from the point of view of the material resources of the state or from that of the preparation of the proletariat itself. We can escape the deadlock at present only by the creation of model communities. The ground beneath our feet must be strengthened step by step; there must be no rushing too far ahead or lapsing into bureaucratic fanciful experiments. At a given moment, the state will be able, with the help of local Soviets, cooperative units, and so on, to socialize the work done, to widen and deepen it. In this way the human family, in the words of Engels, will "jump from the realm of necessity to the realm of freedom."

A LETTER TO A MOSCOW
WOMEN WORKERS' CELEBRATION AND RALLY

Trotsky's message to a rally of women workers in Moscow was printed in Pravda, *November 28, 1923. It was translated into English by George Saunders and printed in* Intercontinental Press, *March 30, 1970.*

I am greatly aggrieved that a lingering cold prevents me from taking part in your rally celebrating the fifth year of the party's correct and extensive work among women. Allow me to send greetings in written form to the participants in the rally and, through them, to the women workers and peasants whom the party's work has already awakened and those whom it will awaken tomorrow.

The problem of women's emancipation, both material and spiritual, is closely tied to that of the transformation of family life. It is necessary to remove the bars from those confining and suffocating cages into which the present family structure drives woman, turning her into a slave, if not a beast of burden. This can be accomplished only through the organization of communal methods of feeding and child-rearing.

The road to this is not a short one: material resources are necessary; strength of will, knowledge, and effort are necessary.

There are two paths leading to the transformation of everyday family life: from below and from above. "From below" denotes the path of combining the resources and efforts of individual families, the path of building enlarged family units with kitchens, laundries, etc., in common. "From above" denotes the path of initiative by the state or by local Soviets in building group workers' quarters, communal restaurants, laundries, nurseries, etc. Between these two paths, in a workers' and peasants' state, there can be no contradiction; one ought to supplement the other. The efforts of the state would come to naught without the independent striving toward a new way of life by the workers' families themselves; but even the most energetic display of initiative by individual workers' families, without guidance and aid by the local Soviets and state authorities, could not bring great success either. The work must be carried on simultaneously both from above and from below.

An obstacle in this path, as well as in others, is presented by the scarcity of material resources. But this only means that actual success will not be as rapid as we would have wished. It would be totally inadmissible, however, if on the grounds of poverty we began to brush aside the question of building a new kind of life.

Inertia and blind habit, unfortunately, constitute a great force. And nowhere does blind, dumb habit hold sway with such force as in the dark and secluded inner life of the family. And who is called upon first of all to struggle against the barbaric family situation if not the woman revolutionist? By this I do not mean to say at all that conscious workers are relieved of the responsibility to labor toward the transformation of the economic forms of family life, above all the forms of feeding, child-rearing, and education. But those who fight most energetically and persistently for the *new* are those who suffer most from the *old*. And in the present family situation the one that suffers most is the woman — the wife and the mother.

That is why the proletarian Communist woman — and in her footsteps, every awakened woman — should devote a major part of her strength and attention to the task of transforming our everyday life. If our economic and cultural backwardness creates many difficulties and only permits us to move slowly along this path, still it is necessary that the collective public opinion of all women workers be applied as pressure so that everything that can be done, given our present forces and resources, will be done.

Only in this way will we open up for the most backward and beclouded working woman, and after her the peasant woman, the door to the kingdom of socialism.

I wish you every success in your work.

Yours with Communist greetings,

L. Trotsky

THE PROTECTION OF MOTHERHOOD AND THE STRUGGLE FOR CULTURE

Trotsky addressed the Third All-Union Conference on Protection of Mothers and Children on December 7, 1925. The speech was published in both Pravda *and* Izvestia *December 17, 1925. It was translated by John Fairlie and appears here for the first time in English.*

Comrades, your conference on the protection of mothers and children is valuable because it shows by the content of its activities that work on the construction of the new socialist culture is being carried on from various angles, simultaneously and in a parallel way.

Only yesterday did I have the opportunity to acquaint myself with the theses presented to your conference in pamphlet form — although I hadn't time to go through them thoroughly. And in the theses, what is most striking to one who is observing more or less from the sidelines (although in essence no one has the right to stand aside from your work) is the fact that your work has acquired extraordinary concreteness and depth; from those misty problems which we posed in the years 1918-19 in all fields of our culture and our life, we have already gone over to concrete thinking through and businesslike working out of these problems on the basis of our common experience, without losing the necessary perspectives and without falling into hairsplitting. And this is a great achievement of ours in all fields of our work and is expressed fully and comprehensively in the theses on the protection of mothers and children.

Comrades, what attracted the most attention (at least

mine — and I think this may well apply to every reader
of the theses) — what attracted the most attention was the
table included in the thesis of Comrade Lebedeva on infant mortality. It staggered me. You have probably already discussed this question here more concretely, but,
at the risk of repeating what has already been said, I
must still dwell on this point. We have here a table com-
paring the mortality of infants up to one year old for
1913 and 1923. Is this table true? That is the first question I shall ask myself and shall ask others. Is it true?
In any case, it will be subject to public verification. I
think it ought to be extracted from the theses, which are
available only to you specialized workers in this field,
and be made the fighting property of our press in general — Soviet and party. It must be subjected to statistical clarification and cross-checking, and if it is true,
then it should be recorded as a very valuable achievement in our socialist cultural inventory.

It appears from this table that in 1913, when Russia
was considerably richer than we are now — yes, Russia,
as a state, as a nation, or as a collection of nations, was
considerably richer than we are now (we are now approaching the year 1913 *in production,* but not yet *in
accumulation,* and even when we have fully equalled the
level of industrial and agricultural production of 1913,
it will still be a long time before we have the accumu-
lations of national wealth that there were in 1913) — despite this, it turns out that in 1913 the mortality of infants up to one year was 29 percent in Vladimir province; now it is 17.5 percent. And for Moscow province
it was almost 28 percent; now it is about 14 percent.

Is this true or untrue? [*Voice: true!*] I shall not dare
to dispute that. I only say: you know it; the whole country should learn it. The contrast between these figures
must be carefully checked before all eyes. It is surprising —
such a fall in mortality with such a low level of productive forces and of accumulation in the country. If this
is a fact, then it is the most indisputable achievement
of our new culture of everyday life and, above all, of
your efforts as an organization. If this is a fact, then

it should be proclaimed not only within the Union, but also on a world scale. And if, after checking, this fact becomes indisputable, for public opinion as a whole, then you must solemnly proclaim that from now on we shall cease altogether to make comparisons with the prewar level.

The table shows that in Moscow province infants up to one year old die at a rate half that of before the war. But our cultural and everyday conditions before the war were conditions of lordliness and boorishness, i.e., the most contemptible conditions, the most terrifying conditions. Success with respect to these conditions is very gratifying, but prewar conditions cannot go on being our criterion. We have to seek some other criterion, and for the moment we must still seek this criterion in the civilized *capitalist* world — at what rate do infants die in capitalist Germany, France, England, and America?

And here again I find a complete parallelism of method and similarity of approach to the question — in your work and in everyone else's. If you follow the work of our industry and our agriculture, the same processes may be observed: until yesterday, until today we worked and are working with an eye on the prewar level. We say: our industry in the past year reached 75 percent of the prewar level; this year, starting October 1, it will reach, let us say, 95 percent, and if things go well, even the full 100 percent. But *ipso facto,* we are ceasing to compare our success with the prewar level. We don't have to come up to a prewar level that is becoming part of the history of our barbarism, but we have to equal the pressure — economic, military, and cultural — which is bearing on us from abroad. The capitalist foes are more cultured than we are, more powerful than we are; their industry is superior to ours, and it is possible that despite the capitalist structure that prevails there, the infant mortality in some of them is still lower than here.

It therefore seems to me that this table should become a landmark, marking a turning point in your work. In subjecting this table to verification, in fixing it in the general consciousness, we say: from now on we shall

compare not with the prewar level but with those states
of the highest standing in respect to culture.

The fate of mother and child, speaking schematically,
i.e., about the most basic features, depends in the first
place on the development of the productive forces of a
given society, on the extent of its wealth, and secondly,
on the distribution of this wealth among the members
of the society, i.e., on the social structure. That
state may be capitalist in structure, i.e., be at a lower
social stage than the socialist one, but nevertheless be
richer. This is precisely the case that history now pre-
sents us: the leading capitalist countries are incomparably
richer than we are, but the system of distribution and
consumption of this wealth there belongs to the preceding
period of history, i.e., to capitalism. Our social structure,
by the possibilities contained in it, must seek for itself
criteria, models, goals, and tasks incomparably higher
than those capitalism can provide. But since capitalism
is still incomparably richer than we are in productive
forces, we must take as our *immediate* task to catch up
with it, so as later to outdistance it. That means that
after having overtaken one barrier — the prewar level — we
must assign ourselves a second task — to equal as soon
as possible the best achievements of the most advanced
countries, where the question of mothers and children
of the toilers receives from the bourgeoisie the attention
dictated by its own class interests.

It may be said that if the position of mother and child
depends, in the first instance, on the development of the
productive forces, on the general level of the economy
in a given country, and, secondly, on the social structure,
on the manner of consumption and distribution of the
wealth of a given country, then what significance, you
may ask, has the work of your special organization?
I pose this question rhetorically. Any social structure,
including a socialist one, can find itself faced with the
phenomenon that the material possibilities for a given
improvement and alteration of life are present, but slug-
gishness, lazy habits of thought, servile traditions, conservative stupidity may be met even in the socialist struc-

ture, as a link with the past, as an absence of initiative and boldness in destroying the old form of life. And the task of our party and the series of social organizations led by it, such as yours, consists in pressing forward customs, everyday habits, and psychology, and preventing the conditions of everyday life from falling behind the socioeconomic possibilities.

As far as technology is concerned, there is a big whip here: the pressure from the West. We have come out onto the European market; we are buying and selling. As businessmen, we, i.e., the state, are interested in selling dear and buying cheap, but if you want to buy and sell well, you have to produce cheaply, and to produce cheaply, you have to have good technology and a high level of organization of production. That means that in coming out onto the world market we have placed ourselves under the whip of European and American technology. Here, whether we want to or not, we have to go forward. All the problems of our social structure, and that also means the fate of mothers and children, depend on the success with which we withstand this worldwide competition. That we have settled accounts with the bourgeoisie in our country, that on the basis of NEP our state industry is flourishing and developing, that there is no danger of the private industrialist beating state industry on the market—indisputable figures confirm this—is now clear to all. But once we have come out onto the international market, the competitor here is stronger, more powerful, more educated. Here we have a new standard in the economic field—catching up with European and American technology, so as to surpass it later.

Yesterday we opened a power station 130 kilometers from Moscow—Shatura station. This is a great technical accomplishment. The Shatura station is built on peat, on a bog. There is a considerable quantity of bogs in our country, and if we can learn to transform the latent energy of our bogs into the moving energy of electricity, this will have a beneficial effect on both mothers and children. [*Applause.*] The celebration in honor of the builders of this station gave us at the same time a clear picture of

our whole culture with all its contradictions. We set off
from Moscow. What is Moscow? Delegates from the
provinces, in Moscow for the first time, can see that Moscow is the center of our Soviet Union, a world center of
ideas for leading the working-class movement. Shatura
(a little more than one hundred versts from Moscow)
is a great technical achievement; it is in size and construction the only *peat* power station in the world.

Between Shaturka[5] and Moscow we looked out of the
windows of the train. Forest, slumbering, impassable,
just as it was in the seventeenth century. And hamlets,
scattered here and there, almost the same as they were
in the seventeenth century. Of course the revolution has
raised the culture in these little villages, especially near
Moscow, but how many signs there are still of medievalism, of terrifying backwardness, above all in the question
of mothers and children.

Yes, you have won great victories for the first time in
the villages, for which every conscious citizen of our Union
may congratulate you. But your theses in no way conceal
how much age-old darkness there still is in every village—
even on the road between Moscow and Shaturka. The
villages will have to be urged on to catch up with Moscow and Shaturka, for Shaturka is advanced technology,
based upon electrification. Here we may again remember
the words of V. I. Lenin that socialism is Soviet power
plus electrification.

To urge life on, so that it does not lag behind technical
achievements, is a very important task for you, for everyday life is fearfully conservative, incomparably more conservative than technology. For the peasant man
and woman, for the working man and woman, there are
no first-hand models of the new that would attract them
by force of example, and there is no compelling necessity
for them to follow such models. As far as technology is
concerned, America says to us: "Build Shatura, or we'll
eat up your socialism, bones and all, and leave not a
trace." But daily life seems to have been preserved in a
shell; it does not sense these blows directly, and therefore
the initiative of social work is especially necessary here.

I have already mentioned that in the theses I found out what a great beginning had been made by you in penetrating to the countryside. Here in the theses of E. A. Feder is an indication not only of the colossal need in the village for child-care centers but also of the enormous *response* from the peasantry, i.e., a conscious striving to have these centers in the countryside. But not so long ago — in 1918-19 — there was a great mistrust of them even in the towns. This too is without doubt a great victory, if the new social order has already reached the peasant family from this direction. For the peasant family too will gradually be reconstructed. I would be inclined to dwell longer on this, for even here in the press voices can be heard suggesting that in questions of the family we ought to imitate the worst peasant prejudices, and that this follows from the "smychka."[6] In fact our task is, starting from what exists in the villages — and there exists backwardness and prejudices and darkness which cannot be erased with a stroke of the pen — to find the "smychka," to find the vital hook to which we can attach ourselves and skillfully pull the peasant family forward on the road to the first stages of socialism, but definitely not passively to imitate the existing conceptions and traditions, which are based on slavery.

What is our old culture in the area of the family and everyday life? On top was the nobility, who put the stamp of vulgarity, on a basis of darkness and lack of culture, on all social life. And if our proletariat, which emerged from the peasantry, caught up in a single leap with the European proletariat in some thirty to fifty years and then overtook it in the fields of class struggle and revolutionary politics, there is still, in the proletariat too, more than a little of the foul old leftovers of serfdom in the field of personal morals, the family, and everyday life. And in the intellectual or petty-bourgeois family, you can still find as much as you like of genuine present-day serfdom. You should not set yourself the utopian task of over-turning the old family by some kind of instant juridical leap — you'll fall on your face and compromise yourself in front of the peasantry — but within the material possibilities, within the already assured conditions of social development, act, along the legal line too, so as to direct the family toward the future.

I do not intend at the moment to talk about the projected marriage law, which is under discussion, and about which I reserve the right to speak. I presume that your organization, too, will be taking the proper place in the struggle for a correct law of marriage. I would like to mention only one argument that struck me. The argument is roughly as follows: how can you give the "unwed" mother, i.e., the mother that is not registered, the same rights to help from the father as a "married" mother? Surely that means pushing a woman into the kind of relationship which she would not have entered into if the law denied her this right?

Comrades, this is so monstrous that it makes you wonder: Are we really in a society transforming itself in a socialist manner, i.e., in Moscow or Shaturka, and not somewhere in between Moscow and Shaturka in the slumbering forest? Here the attitude to woman is not only not communist, but reactionary and philistine in the worst sense of the word. Who could think that the rights of woman, who has to bear the consequences of every marital union, however transitory, could be *too* zealously guarded in our country? I think there is no need to demonstrate all the monstrosity of this way of putting the question. But it is symptomatic and bears witness to the fact that in our traditional views, concepts, and customs, there is much that is truly thick-headed and that needs to be smashed with a battering ram.

Fighting for mothers and children in our present conditions means fighting in particular against alcoholism. I unfortunately have not noticed any theses on alcoholism here. [*Voice: There are none.*] Excuse me, I came too late and cannot suggest that this point be placed on the agenda, but I shall request that this question be added to the agenda for your next congress and, more important, to your current work. You cannot fight for the improvement of the position of mother and child without fighting on a wide front against alcoholism.

It says in the theses, and rightly too, that irregular sexual relationships cannot be arbitrarily struck from the books and that powerful social opinion against frequent divorce is necessary, etc. That is correct. But, comrades, in evaluating sexual relationships as frivolous, in many cases it must be said: there is no greater threat than those sexual relationships which are formed under the influence of alcoholism, in drunkenness, and which occur very frequently in a less educated environment. It is your organization which should, in my opinion, take the initiative upon itself in the struggle against drunkenness.

If we split up the question of the fate of mother and child into a series of questions, selecting in particular the fight against drunkenness, then we shall realize clearly that the basic form of struggle for greater stability and rationality in family connections and relationships consists of raising the level of the human personality. Abstract propaganda or preaching will not help this matter. Legislative frameworks in the sense of the protection of the mother in the most difficult periods of her life and the protection of the infant are absolutely necessary, and if we go to extremes in legislation, then of course it will be not towards the father, but towards the mother and child, for the rights of the mother, however they may be assured juridically, will in fact — by virtue of morals, customs, and the role of the mother herself — be insufficiently protected until we arrive at developed socialism, and still more at communism. It is therefore necessary to give as much juridical support as possible to the mother and child, to lead the struggle along various tracks, including against alcoholism. In the very near future this will not be the smallest branch of our work.

But the basic way, I repeat, is to raise the human personality. The higher a man is spiritually, according to the nature of his interests, according to his level, the more he will demand from himself and from his friends, male and female; the more mutual are the demands, the stronger is the connection, the more difficult it is to break. That means the basic task is solved in all fields of our social work by the development of industry, the development of agriculture, welfare, culture, enlightenment. All this leads not to chaotic relationships but on the contrary to more stable ones, which finally will require no legal regulation.

To return to work in the countryside. I think that there is no mention here of our agricultural communes. [*Voice: There is.*] Excuse me, that is my oversight. Not so long ago I visited two large agricultural communes, one in the Zaporozh region, in the Ukraine, the other in the Tersk region in the northern Caucasus. Of course, this is still not the "Shatura" of our way of life, i.e., it cannot be said that this will stand for the new way of family life, as Shatura stands for the new technology, but there are hints here, especially if one compares them with what lies all around them in the countryside. In the commune there are child-care facilities as a regular institution based on cooperative work, as a constituent part of the large family. There is a room for young girls and a room for young boys. In Zaporozh, where an artist was a member of the commune, the walls of the children's rooms are very well decorated with paintings. There is a communal kitchen and dining room and a clubroom-library area. This is really a little child's kingdom in a specially allotted wing of the common house. This is a great step forward by comparison with the peasant family. A woman in the commune can feel herself a human being.

Of course, comrades, I fully realize that, in the first place, this is a small oasis and, in the second place, it is not yet proved that this oasis assures its own extension, for the productivity of labor in these communes is still far from assured. But generally speaking, every social form, every cell will be viable if the productivity of labor in it grows and does not stay on the same level or fall. To construct socialism, to assure the fate of mother and child, is possible only on the basis of the growth of the economy — on the basis of decay and poverty it is possible only to return to medieval barbarism. But the seeds of new possibilities have undoubtedly been demonstrated in the agricultural communes, and they are especially

valuable now, when the development of commodity production in the countryside is giving rise to some extent
to forms of capitalist stratification at the outlying edges
among the kulaks and poor peasants. How much dearer
to us are all forms of cooperation in the countryside, all
collective forms of solving economic, domestic, cultural,
or family problems. The fact that the countryside, as it
says in the theses, is showing support for the child-care
centers, which did not exist up to now, and that this support has started from the poor peasant families and gone
over to middle peasant families, is a fact of colossal significance, if along with it we will have little village "Shaturkas" of production and family and domestic life, i.e.,
agricultural communes, which, it seems to me, must be
taken into your special care, from the point of view of
their family and domestic structure and of the position
of mothers and infants in them.

I was very interested in the attitude of the peasantry toward the commune "Communist Beacon." Beacon is a very
significant word. A beacon is what shows the way, shines
for all from afar. We gave any number of such names
in 1918, but how many of them turned out to be accidental, unfounded, sometimes frivolous "beacons," many
of which have gone out! And therefore it was very important to check this name and see to what extent it was
justified. And it must be said that although this "beacon"
is shining in a region consisting of mainly Cossacks
and partly of religious sects, Baptists, etc. — and these are
all pretty conservative elements — the old hostility to communes has not been shown. That is, it undoubtedly exists
among kulak elements, but since this commune works in
a more or less friendly manner, since this commune has
three tractors, which under appropriate conditions serve
the district as well, through this "smychka" it is accustom-
ing even the surrounding Cossacks to the new forms of
family and domestic life, and the former hostility, I say,
has gone. This is a real gain.

Some comrades have said to me that in some Soviet
circles the attitude is appearing that the agricultural commune is out of place now, ahead of its time; that it is

an anticipation of tomorrow. Not true. The commune
is one of the *embryos* of tomorrow. Of course, the main
work of preparation is carried out along more basic
lines: the development of industry, which will give the
countryside the technical basis for industrialized agriculture; and a cooperative form of distribution of economic
benefits, without which it is impossible to raise the middle peasants to socialism. But along with this, having
such living models of the new economic forms and the
new family and domestic attitudes in the countryside, to
have such family and domestic "Shaturkas," means also
to prepare tomorrow from below, helping to work out
new attitudes toward woman and child.

We Marxists say that the value of a social structure
is determined by the development of productive forces.
This is indisputable. But it is also possible to approach
the problem from the other end. The development of the
productive forces is not needed for its own sake. In the
last analysis the development of the productive forces
is needed because it provides the basis for a new human
personality, conscious, without a lord over him on earth,
not fearing imaginary lords, born of fear, in the sky —
a human personality which absorbs into itself all the
best of what was created by the thought and creativity
of past ages, which in solidarity with all others goes
forward, creates new cultural values, constructs new personal and family attitudes, higher and nobler than those
which were born on the basis of class slavery. The development of the productive forces is dear to us, as the
material presupposition of a higher human personality,
not shut up in itself, but cooperative, associative.

From this point of view it may be said that probably
for many decades to come it will be possible to evaluate
a human society by the attitude it has toward woman, toward the mother and toward the child — and this is true
not only for evaluating society, but also the individual
person. The human psyche does not develop evenly in
all its parts. We are living in a political age, a revolutionary age, when working men and women are developing themselves in a struggle, forming themselves above

all in a revolutionary political way. And those cells of consciousness where family views and traditions reside, and the attitude of one man to another, to woman, to child, and so on — these cells often remain in the old form. The revolution has not yet worked upon them. The cells in the brain in which political and social views reside are being worked upon in our time much more quickly and sharply, thanks to the whole structure of society and thanks to the epoch in which we are living. (Of course, this is only an analogy — in the brain the process works differently.) And therefore we shall go on for a long time observing that we are constructing a new industry, a new society, but in the field of personal relations much still remains from the Middle Ages. And therefore one of the criteria for the evaluation of our culture, and a standard for individual proletarian working men and women and progressive peasants, is the attitude toward woman and the attitude toward the child.

Vladimir Ilyich taught us to value the working-class parties according to their attitude, in particular and in general, toward the oppressed nations, toward the colonies. Why? Because if you take, say, the English worker, it is much easier to arouse in him the feeling of solidarity with his whole class — he will take part in strikes and will even arrive at revolution — but to make him raise himself to solidarity with a yellow-skinned Chinese coolie, to treat him as a brother in exploitation, will prove much more difficult, since here it is necessary to break through a shell of national arrogance which has been built up over centuries.

And just so, comrades, has the shell of family prejudices, in the attitudes of the head of the family toward woman and child — and woman is the coolie of the family — this shell has been laid down over millenia, and not centuries. And thus you are — you must be — the moral battering ram which will break through this shell of conservatism, rooted in our old Asiatic nature, in slavery, in serfdom, in bourgeois prejudices, and in the prejudices of the workers themselves, which have arisen from the worst aspects of peasant traditions. Inasmuch as you will be destroying this shell, like a battering ram in the hands of the socialist society that is being built, every conscious revolutionary, every Communist, every progressive worker and peasant is obliged to support you with all his might. I wish you great success, comrades, and above all I wish you more attention from our public opinion. Your work, which is really purifying, really salutary, must be placed in the center of attention of our press, so that it can be supported on the shoulders of all progressive elements in the country, and you can be helped to reach successes in the reconstruction of our way of life and culture. [*Loud applause.*]

TO BUILD SOCIALISM MEANS TO EMANCIPATE WOMEN AND PROTECT MOTHERS

This article first appeared in Za Novyi Byt *in December 1925. It was translated by John Fairlie and appears here for the first time in English.*

The most accurate way of measuring our advance is by the practical measures which are being carried out for the improvement of the position of mother and child. This index is very reliable; it does not deceive. It immediately shows both the material successes and the cultural achievements in the broad sense. Historical experience shows that even the proletariat, already struggling with the oppressors, is far from prompt in concentrating the necessary attention on the oppressed position of woman as housewife, mother, and wife. Such is the terrible force of being accustomed to the family slavery of woman! There is no point in even talking about the peasantry. The burden and hopelessness of the fate of the peasant woman, and not only from poor but even from middle families, can probably not be compared today even with the worst penal servitude. No rest, no holiday, no gleam of hope! Our revolution is only gradually reaching down to the familial foundations, mainly in the towns, for the moment, in the industrial regions, and only very slowly is it penetrating into the countryside. And the problems here are immeasurable.

To alter the position of woman *at the root* is possible only if all the conditions of social, family, and domestic existence are altered. The depth of the question of the mother is expressed in the fact that she is, in essence, a living point where all the decisive strands of economic and cultural work intersect. The question of motherhood is above all a question of an apartment, running water, a kitchen, a laundry room, a dining room. But it is just as much a question of a school, of books, of a place for recreation. Drunkenness beats down most mercilessly on the housewife and mother. Illiteracy and unemployment also. Running water and electricity in the apartment lighten the woman's burden above all.

Motherhood is the question of all questions. Here all the strands come together and from here they again go out in all directions. The undoubted growth of material sufficiency in the country makes it possible, and therefore also necessary, to carry consideration for mother and child incomparably wider and deeper than hitherto. The degree of our energy in this field will show to what extent we have learned to link ends with ends in the basic questions of our life.

Just as it was impossible to approach the construction of the Soviet state without freeing the peasantry from the tangles of serfdom, so it is impossible to move to socialism without freeing the peasant woman and the woman worker from the bondage of family and household. And if we used to determine the maturity of a revolutionary worker not only by his attitude to the capitalist but also by his attitude to the peasant, i. e., by his understanding of the necessity of freeing the peasant from bondage — so now we can and must measure the socialist maturity of the worker and the progressive peasant by their attitude to woman and child, by their understanding of the necessity of freeing from bondage the mother in penal servitude, of giving her the possibility of straightening her back and involving herself as she should in social and cultural life.

Motherhood is the hub of all problems. That is why each new measure, each law, each practical step in economic and social construction must also be checked against the question of how it will affect the family, whether it worsens or lightens the fate of the mother, whether it improves the position of the child.

The great number of homeless children in our towns bears most terrible witness to the fact that we are still caught up on all sides in the tangles of the old society, which manifests itself in the most vicious way in the epoch of its downfall. The position of mother and child was never so difficult as in the years of the transition from the old to the new, especially in the years of the civil war. The intervention of Clemenceau and Churchill and the Kolchak, Denikin, and Wrangel elements[7] hit most cruelly at the woman worker, at the peasant woman, at the mother, and left us an inheritance of unprecedented child homelessness. The child is from the mother and the homelessness of the child is above all the fruit of maternal homelessness. Consideration for the mother is the truest and deepest way to the improvement of the fate of the child.

The general growth of the economy is creating the conditions for a gradual reconstruction of family and domestic life. All questions connected with this must be posed in their full magnitude. We are approaching from various directions the renewal of the basic capital of the country; we are acquiring new machines to replace the old ones; we are building new factories; we are renewing our railways; the peasant is acquiring plows, seeders, tractors.

But the most basic "capital" is the people, i.e., its strength, its health, its cultural level. This capital requires renewal even more than the equipment of the factories or the peasant implements. It must not be thought that the ages of slavery, hunger, and bondage, the years of war and epidemics, have passed without a trace. No, they have left behind in the living organism of the people both wounds and scars. Tuberculosis, syphilis, neurasthenia, alcoholism—all these diseases and many others are spread widely among the masses of the population. The nation must be made healthy. Without that, socialism is unthinkable.

We must reach the roots, the sources. And where is the source of the nation if not in the mother? The struggle against the neglect of mothers must be given first place! Housing construction, the construction of child-care facilities, kindergartens, communal dining rooms and laundries must be put in the center of attention, and that attention must be vigilant and well organized. Here questions of *quality* decide all. Child-care, eating and laundry facilities must be set up so that by the advantages they pro-

vide they can deal a deathblow to the old closed-in, isolated family unit, completely supported on the bent
shoulders of the housewife and mother. Improvement of
the environment inevitably calls forth a surge of demand,
and then a surge of means. Caring for children in public
facilities, as well as feeding of adults in communal canteens, is cheaper than in the family. But the transfer of
material means from the family to the child-care centers
and canteens will take place only if the social organization learns to satisfy the most primary demands better
than the family. Special attention must now be paid to
the questions of quality. Vigilant social control and con-
stant urging on all the organs and institutions which
serve the family and domestic needs of the toiling masses
is essential.

The initiators in the great struggle for the liberation
of mothers must of course be the advanced women workers. At all costs this movement must be directed against
the village. In our city life too, there is still much of the
petty-bourgeois-peasant character. The view of women
held by many working men is still not socialist, but conservative, peasant, essentially medieval. Thus the peasant
mother oppressed by the yoke of the family pulls the worker mother down with her. The peasant woman must be
raised up. She must desire to raise herself, i. e., she must
be awakened and shown the way.

It is impossible to move forward while leaving the woman far in the rear. Woman is the mother of the nation.
From the enslavement of women grow prejudices and
superstitions which shroud the children of the new generation and penetrate deeply into all the pores of the national consciousness. The best and most profound path
of struggle against the superstition of religion is the path
of all-sided concern for the mother. She must be raised
up and enlightened. Freeing the mother means cutting
the last umbilical cord linking the people with the dark
and superstitious past.

FAMILY RELATIONS UNDER THE SOVIETS

This article was published under the title "Is Soviet Russia Fit to Recognize?" in the January 14, 1933, issue of Liberty *magazine. Trotsky's answers, written in English, were to fourteen questions submitted to him by* Liberty *in advance.*

The question of recognizing the Soviet Union is now being widely discussed in the United States. Diplomatic recognition, naturally, does not mean that each side approves the politics of the other. The non-recognition of the Soviet Republic up to now has chiefly been based on reasons of a moral nature. The questions put to me by the editor of *Liberty* cover these grounds.

1. Does the Soviet state turn men into robots?
Why? I ask. The ideologists of the patriarchal system, like Tolstoy or Ruskin, object that machine civilization turns the free peasant and craftsman into joyless automatons. In the last decades this charge has mostly been leveled against the industrial system of America (Taylorism, Fordism).

Shall we now, perhaps, hear from Chicago and Detroit the outcry against the soul-destroying machine? Why not return to stone hatchets and mud dwellings, why not go back to sheepskin coverings? No; we refuse to do that. In the field of mechanization the Soviet Republic is so far only a disciple of the United States — and has no intention of stopping halfway.

But perhaps the question is aimed not at mechanical operation but at the distinctive features of the social order. Are not men becoming robots in the Soviet state because the machines are state property and not private-

ly owned? It is enough to ask the question clearly to show
that it has no foundation.

There remains, finally, the question of the political regime, the hard dictatorship, the highest tension of all
forces, the low standard of living of the population. There
would be no sense in denying these facts. But they are the
expression not so much of the new regime as of the fear-
ful inheritance of backwardness.

The dictatorship will have to become softer and milder
as the economic welfare of the country is raised. The present method of *commanding human beings* will give way
to one of *disposing over things.* The road leads not to
the robot but to man of a higher order.

2. *Is the Soviet State completely dominated by a small
group in the Kremlin who exercise oligarchical powers
under the guise of a dictatorship of the proletariat?*

No, that is not so. The same class can rule with the
help of different political systems and methods according to circumstances. So the bourgeoisie on its historical
road carried through its rule under absolute monarchy,
Bonapartism, [8] parliamentary republic, and fascist dictatorship. All these forms of rule retain a capitalist character
insofar as the most important riches of the nation, the administration of the means of production, of the schools,
and of the press, remain united in the hands of the bourgeoisie, and insofar as the laws first of all protect bourgeois property.

The Soviet regime means the rule of the proletariat,
irrespective of how broad the stratum in whose hands
the power is *immediately concentrated.*

3. *Have the Soviets robbed childhood of joy and turned
education into a system of Bolshevist propaganda?*

The education of children has always and everywhere
been connected with propaganda. The propaganda begins
by instilling the advantages of a handkerchief over the fin-
gers, and rises to the advantages of the Republican platform over the Democratic, or vice versa. Education in the
spirit of religion is propaganda; you will surely not refuse

to admit that St. Paul was one of the greatest of propagandists.

The worldly education supplied by the French Republic is soaked with propaganda to the marrow. Its main idea is that all virtue is inherent in the French nation or, more accurately, in the ruling class of the French nation.

No one can possibly deny that the education of Soviet children, too, is propaganda. The only difference is that in bourgeois countries it is a question of injecting into the child respect for *old* institutions and ideas which are taken for granted. In the USSR it is a question of new ideas, and therefore the propaganda leaps to the eye. "Propaganda," in the evil sense of the word, is the name that people usually give to the defense and spread of such ideas as do not please them.

In times of conservatism and stability, the daily propaganda is not noticeable. In times of revolution, propaganda necessarily takes on a belligerent and aggressive character. When I returned to Moscow from Canada with my family early in May 1917, my two boys studied at a "gymnasium" [roughly, high school] which was attended by the children of many politicians, including some ministers of the provisional government. In the whole gymnasium there were only two Bolsheviks, my sons and a third sympathizer. In spite of the official rule, "the school must be free of politics," my son, barely twelve years old, was unmercifully beaten up as a Bolshevik. After I was elected chairman of the Petrograd Soviet, my son was never called anything but "chairman" and received a double beating. That was propaganda against Bolshevism.

Those parents and teachers who are devoted to the old society cry out against "propaganda." If a state is to build a new society, can it do otherwise than begin with the school?

"Does the Soviet propaganda rob childhood of joy?" For what reason and in what manner? Soviet children play, sing, dance, and cry like all other children. The unusual care of the Soviet regime for the child is admit-

ted even by malevolent observers. Compared with the
old regime, infant mortality has declined by half.

It is true, Soviet children are told nothing about original sin and Paradise. In this sense one may say that
the children are being robbed of the joys of life after
death. Being no expert in these matters, I dare not judge
the extent of the loss. Still, the pains of this life take a
certain precedence over the joys of the life to come. If
children absorb the necessary quantity of calories, the
abundance of their living forces will find reasons enough
for joy.

Two years ago my five-year-old grandson came to me
from Moscow. Although he knew nothing whatever about
God, I could find no particularly sinful inclinations in
him, except for the time when with the help of some newspapers, he succeeded in hermetically sealing up the wash-
basin drainpipe. In order to have him mingle with other
children on Prinkipo, we had to send him to a kindergarten conducted by Catholic nuns. The worthy sisters
have nothing but praise for the morals of my now nearly
seven-year-old atheist.

Thanks to this same grandchild, I have been able in
the past year to make a fairly close acquaintance with
Russian children's books, those of the Soviets as well
as of the emigres. There is propaganda in both. Yet the
Soviet books are incomparably fresher, more active, more
full of life. The little man reads and listens to these books
with the greatest pleasure. No, Soviet propaganda does
not rob childhood of joy.

4. Is Bolshevism deliberately destroying the family?
*5. Is Bolshevism subversive of all moral standards
in sex?*
*6. Is it true that bigamy and polygamy are not pun-
ishable under the Soviet system?*

If one understands by "family" a compulsory union
based on the marriage contract, the blessing of the church,
property rights, and the single passport, then Bolshevism
has destroyed this policed family from the roots up.

If one understands by "family" the unbounded domina-
tion of parents over children, and absence of legal rights

for the wife, then Bolshevism has, unfortunately, not yet completely destroyed this carryover of society's old barbarism.

If one understands by "family" ideal monogamy—not in the legal but in the actual sense—then the Bolsheviks could not destroy what never was nor is on earth, barring fortunate exceptions.

There is absolutely no foundation for the statement that the Soviet law on marriage has been an incentive to polygamy and polyandry. Statistics of marriage relations—actual ones—are not available, and cannot be. But even without columns of figures one can be sure that the Moscow index numbers of adulteries and shipwrecked marriages are not much different from the corresponding data for New York, London, or Paris, and—who knows?—are perhaps even lower.

Against prostitution there has been a strenuous and fairly successful struggle. This proves that the Soviets have no intention of tolerating that unbridled promiscuity which finds its most destructive and poisonous expression in prostitution.

A long and permanent marriage, based on mutual love and cooperation—that is the ideal standard. The influences of the school, of literature, and of public opinion in the Soviets tend toward this. Freed from the chains of police and clergy, later also from those of economic necessity, the tie between man and woman will find its own way, determined by physiology, psychology, and care for the welfare of the human race. The Soviet regime is still far from the solution of this, among other problems, but it has created serious prerequisites for a solution. In any case, the problem of marriage has ceased to be a matter of uncritical tradition and the blind force of circumstance; it has been posed as a task of collective reason.

Every year five and a half million children are born in the Soviet Union. The excess of births over deaths amounts to more than three million. Czarist Russia knew no such growth in population. This fact alone makes it impossible to speak of moral disintegration or of a lowering of the vital forces of the population of Russia.

7. *Is it true that incest is not regarded as a criminal offense?*

I must admit that I have never taken an interest in this question from the standpoint of criminal prosecution, so that I could not answer without obtaining information as to what the Soviet law says about incest, if it says anything at all. Still, I think the whole question belongs rather to the domain of pathology on the one hand, and education on the other, rather than that of criminology. Incest lessens the desirable qualities and the ability to survive of the human race. For that very reason it is regarded by the great majority of healthy human beings as a violation of normal standards.

The aim of socialism is to bring reason not only into economic relations but also as much as possible into the biological functions of man. Already today the Soviet schools are making many efforts to enlighten the children as to the real needs of the human body and the human spirit. I have no reason to believe that the pathological cases of incest are more numerous in Russia than in other countries. At the same time, I am inclined to hold that precisely in this field judicial intervention can do more harm than good. I question, for example, that humanity would have been the gainer if British justice had sent Byron to jail.

8. *Is it true that a divorce may be had for the asking?*

Of course it is true. It would have been more in place to ask another question: "Is it true that there are still countries where divorce cannot be obtained for the asking by either party to a marriage?"

9. *Is it true that the Soviets have no respect for chastity in men and women?*

I think that in this field it is not respect but hypocrisy that has declined.

Is there any doubt, for example, that Ivar Krueger, the match king, described as a dour ascetic in his lifetime and as an irreconcilable enemy of the Soviets, more than once denounced the immorality of the Russian Komsomol boys and girls who did not seek the blessing of the church on their embraces? Had it not been for the financial wreck, Kreuger would have gone to his grave not only as a just man on the Stock Exchange but also as a pillar of morality. But now the press reports that the number of women kept by Kreuger in various continents was several times the number of the chimneys of his match factories.

French, English, and American novels describe double and triple families not as an exception but as the rule. A very well informed young German observer, Klaus Mehnert, who recently had a book published on the Soviet youth, writes, "It is true the young Russians are no paragons of virtue . . . but morally they are certainly no lower than Germans of the same age." I believe that this is true.

In New York, in February 1917, I observed one evening in a subway car about two dozen students and their girl friends. Although there were a number of people in the car who were not in their party, the conduct of these most vivacious couples was such that one could say at once: even if these young people believe in monogamy in principle, in practice they come to it by devious paths.

The abolition of the American dry law would by no means signify that the new administration was striving to encourage drunkenness. In the same way, the Soviet Government's abolition of a number of laws which were supposed to protect the domestic hearth, chastity, etc., has nothing to do with any effort to destroy the permanence of the family or encourage promiscuity. It is simply a question of attaining, by raising the material and cultural level, something that cannot be attained by formal prohibition or lifeless preaching.

10. Is the ultimate object of Bolshevism to reproduce the beehive or the ant stage in human life?

11. In what respect does the ideal of Bolshevism differ from the state of civilization that would prevail on earth if insects had secured control?

Both questions are unfair to the insects as well as to man. Neither ants nor bees have to answer for such monstrosities as fill human history. On the other hand, no matter how bad human beings may be, they have possibilities which no insect can reach. It would not be difficult to prove that the task of the Soviets is precisely this — to destroy the ant characteristics of human society.

The fact is, bees as well as ants have classes: some work or fight, others specialize in reproduction. Can one see in such a specialization of social functions the ideal of Bolshevism? These are rather the characteristics of our present-day civilization carried to the limit. Certain species of ants make slaves of brother ants of different color.

The Soviet system does not resemble this at all. The ants have not yet even produced their John Brown or Abraham Lincoln.

Benjamin Franklin described man as "the tool-making animal." This notable characterization is at the bottom of the Marxist interpretation of history. The artificial tool has released man from the animal kingdom and has given impetus to the work of the human intellect; it has caused the changes from slavery to feudalism, capitalism, and the Soviet system.

The meaning of the question is clearly that a universal all-embracing control must kill individuality. The evil of the Soviet system would then consist in its excessive control, would it not? Yet a series of other questions, as we have seen, accuses the Soviets of refusal to bring under state control the most intimate fields of personal life — love, family, sex relations. The contradiction is perfectly evident.

The Soviets by no means make it their task to put under control the intellectual and the moral powers of man. On the contrary, through control of conomic life they want to free every human personality from the control of the market and its blind forces.

Ford organized automobile production on the conveyor system and thereby obtained an enormous output. The task of socialism, when one gets down to the principle of productive technique, is to organize the entire national and international economy on the conveyor system, on the basis of a plan and of an accurate proportionment of its parts. The conveyor principle, transferred from single factories to all factories and farms, must result in such an output performance that, compared with it, Ford's achievement will look like a miserable handicraft shop alongside of Detroit. Once man has conquered nature, he will no longer have to earn his daily bread by the sweat of his brow. That is the prerequisite for the liberation of personality.

As soon as three or four hours, let us say, of daily labor suffice to satisfy liberally all material wants, every man and woman will have twenty hours left over, free of all "control." Questions of education, of perfecting the bodily and spiritual structure of man, will occupy the center of general attention. The philosophical and scientific schools, the opposing tendencies in literature, architecture, and art in general, will for the first time be of vital concern not merely to a top layer but to the whole mass of the population. Freed from the pressure of blind economic forces, the struggle of groups, tendencies, and schools will take on a profoundly ideal and unselfish character. In this atmosphere human personality will not dry up, but on the contrary for the first time will come to full bloom.

12. *Is it true that Sovietism teaches children not to respect their parents?*

No; in such a general form this assertion is a mere caricature. Still, it is true that rapid progress in the realms of technique, ideas, or manners generally diminishes the authority of the older generation, including that of parents. When professors lecture on the Darwinian theory, the authority of those parents who believe that Eve was made from Adam's rib can only decline.

In the Soviet Union all conflicts are incomparably sharper and more painful. The mores of the Komsomols must inevitably collide with the authority of the parents who would still like to use their own good judgment in marrying off their sons and daughters. The Red Army man who has learned how to handle tractors and combines cannot acknowledge the technical authority of his father who works with a wooden plow.

To maintain his dignity, the father can no longer merely point with his hand to the icon and reinforce this gesture with a slap on the face. The parents resort to spiritual weapons. The children who base themselves on the official authority of the school show themselves, however, to be the better armed. The injured amour propre of the parents often turns against the state. This usually happens in those families which are hostile to the new regime in its fundamental tasks. The majority of proletarian parents reconcile themselves to the loss of part of their parental authority more readily as the state takes over the greater part of their parental cares. Still, there are conflicts of the generations even in these circles. Among the peasants they take on special sharpness. Is this good or bad? I think it is good. Otherwise there would be no going forward.

Permit me to point to my own experience. At seventeen I had to break away from home. My father had attempted to determine the course of my life. He told me, "Even in three hundred years the things you are aiming for will not come to pass." And, at that, it was only a question of the overthrowing of the monarchy. Later my father understood the limits of his influence and my relations with my family were restored. After the October Revolution he saw his mistake. "Your truth was stronger," he said. Such examples were counted by the thousand; later on, by hundreds of thousands and millions. They characterize the critical upheaval of a period when "the bond of ages" goes to pieces.

13. Is it true that Bolshevism penalizes religion and outlaws religious worship?

This deliberately deceptive assertion has been refuted a thousand times by completely indisputable facts, proofs, and testimony of witnesses. Why does it always come up anew? Because the church considers itself persecuted when it is not supported by the budget and the police force and when its opponents are not subject to the reprisals of persecution.

In many states the scientific criticism of religious faiths is considered a crime; in others it is merely tolerated.

The Soviet state acts otherwise. Far from considering religious worship a crime, it tolerates the existence of various religions, but at the same time openly supports materialist propaganda against religious belief. It is precisely this situation which the church interprets as religious persecution.

14. Is it true that the Bolshevist state, while hostile to religion, nevertheless capitalizes on the prejudices of the ignorant masses? For instance, the Russians do not consider any saint truly acceptable to heaven unless his body defies decomposition. Is that the reason why the Bolshevists artificially preserve the mummy of Lenin?

No; this is a wholly incorrect interpretation, dictated by prejudice and hostility. I can make this statement all the more freely because from the very beginning I have been a determined opponent of the embalming, mausoleum, and the rest, as was also Lenin's widow, N. K. Krupskaya. There is no doubt whatever that if Lenin on his sick bed had thought for a moment that they would treat his corpse like that of a Pharaoh, he would have appealed in advance, with indignation, to the party. I brought this objection forward as my main argument. The body of Lenin must not be used against the spirit of Lenin.

I also pointed to the fact that the "incorruptibility" of the embalmed corpse of Lenin might nourish religious superstitions. Krassin, [9] who defended and apparently initiated the idea of the embalming, objected: "On the contrary, what was a matter of miracle with the priests will become a matter of technology in our hands. Millions of people will have an idea of how the man looked who brought such great changes into the life of our country. With the help of science, we will satisfy this justifiable interest of the masses and at the same time explain to them the mystery of incorruptibility."

Undeniably the erection of the mausoleum had a political aim: to strengthen the authority of the disciples eternally through the authority of the teacher. Still, there is no ground to see in this a capitalization of religious superstition. The mausoleum visitors are told that the credit for the preservation of the body from decomposition is due to chemistry.

Our answers absolutely do not attempt to gloss over the present situation in the Soviet Union, to underestimate the economic and cultural achievements, nor still less to represent socialism as a stage which has already been reached. The Soviet regime is and will remain for a long time a transitional regime, full of contradiction and extreme difficulties. Still, we must take the facts in the light of their development. The Soviet Union took over the inheritance of the Romanov empire. For fifteen years it has lived surrounded by a hostile world.

The situation of a besieged fortress has given the dictatorship particularly crude forms. The policies of Japan are least of all calculated to develop in Russia a feeling of security; but also the fact that the United States, which carried on war against the Soviets on Soviet territory, has not taken up diplomatic relations with Moscow to this very day, has had an enormous and, naturally, negative influence on the internal regime of the country.

THERMIDOR IN THE FAMILY 10

This article is an excerpt from The Revolution Betrayed, *which Trotsky wrote in Norway in 1936. The English translation by Max Eastman was printed in 1937.*

The October Revolution honestly fulfilled its obligations in relation to woman. The young government not only gave her all political and legal rights in equality with man, but, what is more important, did all that it could, and in any case incomparably more than any other government ever did, actually to secure her access to all forms of economic and cultural work. However, the boldest revolution, like the "all-powerful" British Parliament, cannot convert a woman into a man—or rather, cannot divide equally between them the burden of pregnancy, birth, nursing, and the rearing of children.

The revolution made a heroic effort to destroy the so-called family hearth—that archaic, stuffy, and stagnant institution in which the woman of the toiling classes performs galley labor from childhood to death. The place of the family as a shut-in petty enterprise was to be occupied, according to the plans, by a finished system of social care and accommodation: maternity houses, child-care centers, kindergartens, schools, social dining rooms, social laundries, first-aid stations, hospitals, sanatoria, athletic organizations, moving-picture theaters, etc. The complete absorption of the housekeeping functions of the family by institutions of the socialist society, uniting all generations in solidarity and mutual aid, was to bring to woman, and thereby to the loving couple, a real liberation from the thousand-year-old fetters.

Up to now this problem of problems has not been solved. The forty million Soviet families remain in their

overwhelming majority nests of medievalism, female slavery and hysteria, daily humiliation of children, feminine
and childish superstition. We must permit ourselves no
illusions on this account. For that very reason, the con-
secutive changes in the approach to the problem of the
family in the Soviet Union best of all characterize the
actual nature of Soviet society and the evolution of its
ruling stratum.

It proved impossible to take the old family by storm —
not because the will was lacking, and not because the
family was so firmly rooted in men's hearts. On the contrary, after a short period of distrust of the government
and its child-care facilities, kindergartens, and like institutions, the working women, and after them the more
advanced peasants, appreciated the immeasurable advantages of the collective care of children as well as the socialization of the whole family economy. Unfortunately
society proved too poor and little cultured. The real resources of the state did not correspond to the plans and
intentions of the Communist Party. You cannot "abolish"
the family; you have to replace it. The actual liberation
of women is unrealizable on a basis of "generalized want."
Experience soon proved this austere truth which Marx
had formulated eighty years before.

During the lean years the workers, wherever possible,
and in part their families, ate in the factory and other social dining rooms, and this fact was officially regarded as
a transition to a socialist form of life. There is no need of
pausing again upon the peculiarities of the different
periods: military communism, the NEP, and the first five-
year plan.[11]   The fact is that from the moment of the
abolition of the food-card system in 1935, all the better-
placed workers began to return to the home dining table.
It would be incorrect to regard this retreat as a condemnation of the socialist system, which in general was never
tried out. But so much the more withering was the judgment of the workers and their wives upon the "social feeding" organized by the bureaucracy. The same conclusion
must be extended to the social laundries, where they tear
and steal linen more than they wash it. Back to the family
hearth!

But home cooking, and the home washtub, which are now half shamefacedly celebrated by orators and journalists, mean the return of the workers' wives to their pots and pans — that is, to the old slavery. It is doubtful if the resolution of the Communist International on the "complete and irrevocable triumph of socialism in the Soviet Union" sounds very convincing to the women of the factory districts!

The rural family, bound up not only with home industry but with agriculture, is infinitely more stable and conservative than that of the town. Only a few, and as a general rule, anemic agricultural communes introduced social dining rooms and child-care facilities in the first period. Collectivization, according to the first announcements, was to initiate a decisive change in the sphere of the family. Not for nothing did they expropriate the peasant's chickens as well as his cows. There was no lack, at any rate, of announcements about the triumphal march of social dining rooms throughout the country. But when the retreat began, reality suddenly emerged from the shadow of this bragging.

The peasant gets from the collective farm, as a general rule, only bread for himself and fodder for his stock. Meat, dairy products, and vegetables, he gets almost entirely from the adjoining private lots. And once the most important necessities of life are acquired by the isolated efforts of the family, there can no longer be any talk of social dining rooms. Thus the midget farms, creating a new basis for the domestic hearthstone, lay a double burden upon woman.

The total number of steady accommodations in the child-care centers amounted in 1932 to 600,000, and of seasonal accommodations solely during work in the fields to only about 4,000,000. In 1935 the cots numbered 5,600,-000, but the steady ones were still only an insignificant part of the total. Moreover, the existing child-care facilities, even in Moscow, Leningrad, and other centers, are not satisfactory as a general rule to the least fastidious demands. "A child-care center in which the child feels worse than he does at home is not a child-care center but a bad orphan asylum," complains a leading Soviet newspaper.

It is no wonder if the better-placed workers' families avoid child-care facilities. But for the fundamental mass of the toilers, the number even of these "bad orphan asylums" is insignificant. Just recently the Central Executive Committee introduced a resolution that foundlings and orphans should be placed in private hands for bringing up. Through its highest organ, the bureaucratic government thus acknowledged its bankruptcy in relation to the most important socialist function.

The number of children in kindergartens rose during the five years 1930-35 from 370,000 to 1,181,000. The lowness of the figure for 1930 is striking, but the figure for 1935 also seems only a drop in the ocean of Soviet families. A further investigation would undoubtedly show that the principal and, in any case, the better part of these kindergartens appertain to families of the administration, the technical personnel, the Stakhanovists, [12] etc.

The same Central Executive Committee was not long ago compelled to testify openly that the "resolution on the liquidation of homeless and uncared-for children is being weakly carried out." What is concealed behind this dispassionate confession? Only by accident, from newspaper remarks printed in small type, do we know that in Moscow more than a thousand children are living in "extraordinarily difficult conditions"; that in the so-called children's homes of the capital there are about 1,500 children who have nowhere to go and are turned out into the streets; that during the two autumn months of 1935 in Moscow and Leningrad "7,500 parents were brought to court for leaving their children without supervision." What good did it do to bring them to court? How many thousand parents have avoided going to court? How many children in "extraordinarily difficult conditions" remained unrecorded? In what do *extraordinarily* difficult conditions differ from *simply* difficult ones? Those are the questions which remain unanswered. A vast amount of the homelessness of children, obvious and open as well as disguised, is a direct result of the great social crisis in the course of which the old family continues to dissolve far faster than the new institutions are capable of replacing it.

From these same accidental newspaper remarks and from episodes in the criminal records, the reader may find out about the existence in the Soviet Union of prostitution — that is, the extreme degradation of woman in the interests of men who can pay for it. In the autumn of the past year [1935] *Izvestia* suddenly informed its readers, for example, of the arrest in Moscow of "as many as a thousand women who were secretly selling themselves on the streets of the proletarian capital." Among those arrested were 177 working women, ninety-two clerks, five university students, etc. What drove them to the sidewalks? Inadequate wages, want, the necessity to "get a little something for a dress, for shoes."

We should vainly seek the approximate dimensions of this social evil. The modest bureaucracy orders the statistician to remain silent. But that enforced silence itself testifies unmistakably to the numerousness of the "class" of Soviet prostitutes. Here there can be essentially no question of "relics of the past"; prostitutes are recruited from the younger generation. No reasonable person, of course, would think of placing special blame for this sore, as old as civilization, upon the Soviet regime. But it is unforgivable in the presence of prostitution to talk about the triumph of socialism. The newspapers assert, to be sure — insofar as they are permitted to touch upon this ticklish theme — that "prostitution is decreasing." It is possible that this is really true by comparison with the years of hunger and decline (1931-33). But the restoration of money relations which has taken place since then, abolishing all direct rationing, will inevitably lead to a new growth of prostitution as well as of homeless children. Wherever there are privileged, there are pariahs!

The mass homelessness of children is undoubtedly the most unmistakable and most tragic symptom of the difficult situation of the mother. On this subject even the optimistic *Pravda* is sometimes compelled to make a bitter confession: "The birth of a child is for many women a serious menace to their position." It is just for this reason that the revolutionary power gave women the right to abortion, which in conditions of want and family distress, whatever may be said upon this subject by the eunuchs and old maids of both sexes, is one of her most important civil, political, and cultural rights. However, this right of women too, gloomy enough in itself, is under the existing social inequality being converted into a privilege. Bits of information trickling into the press about the practice of abortion are literally shocking. Thus through only one village hospital in one district of the Urals, there passed in 1935 "195 women mutilated by midwives"— among them thirty-three working women, twenty-eight clerical workers, sixty-five collective farm women, fifty-eight housewives, etc. This Ural district differs from the majority of other districts only in that information about it happened to get into the press. How many women are mutilated every day throughout the extent of the Soviet Union?

Having revealed its inability to serve women who are compelled to resort to abortion with the necessary medical aid and sanitation, the state makes a sharp change of course and takes the road of prohibition. And just as in other situations, the bureaucracy makes a virtue of necessity. One of the members of the highest Soviet court, Soltz, a specialist on matrimonial questions, bases the forthcoming prohibition of abortion on the fact that in a socialist society where there are no unemployed, etc., etc., a woman has no right to decline "the joys of motherhood." The philosophy of a priest endowed also with the powers of a gendarme. We just heard from the central organ of the ruling party that the birth of a child is for many women, and it would be truer to say for the overwhelming majority, "a menace to their position." We just heard from the highest Soviet institution that "the liquidation of homeless and uncared for children is being weakly carried out," which undoubtedly means a new increase of homelessness. But here the highest Soviet judge informs us that in a country where "life is happy" abortion should be punished with imprisonment— just exactly as in capitalist countries where life is grievous.

It is clear in advance that in the Soviet Union as in the West those who will fall into the claws of the jailer will be chiefly working women, servants, peasant wives, who find it hard to conceal their troubles. As far as concerns "our women," who furnish the demand for fine perfumes and other pleasant things, they will, as formerly, do what they find necessary under the very nose of an indulgent justiciary. "We have need of people," concludes Soltz, closing his eyes to the homeless. "Then have the kindness to bear them yourselves," might be the answer of millions of toiling women to the high judge, if the bureaucracy had not sealed their lips with the seal of silence. These gentlemen have, it seems, completely forgotten that socialism was to remove the cause which impels woman to abortion and not force her into the "joys of motherhood" with the help of a foul police interference in what is to every woman the most intimate sphere of life.

The draft of the law forbidding abortion was submitted to so-called universal popular discussion, and even through the fine sieve of the Soviet press many bitter complaints and stifled protests broke out. The discussion was cut off as suddenly as it had been announced, and on June 27 the Central Executive Committee converted the shameful draft into a thrice shameful law. Even some of the official apologists of the bureaucracy were embarrassed. Louis Fischer[13] declared this piece of legislation something in the nature of a deplorable misunderstanding. In reality the new law against women — with an exception in favor of ladies — is the natural and logical fruit of a Thermidorean reaction.

The triumphal rehabilitation of the family, taking place simultaneously — what a providential coincidence! — with the rehabilitation of the ruble, is caused by the material and cultural bankruptcy of the state. Instead of openly saying, "We have proven still too poor and ignorant for the creation of socialist relations among men, our children and grandchildren will realize this aim," the leaders are forcing people to glue together again the shell of the broken family, and not only that, but to consider it, under threat of extreme penalties, the sacred nucleus of triumphant socialism. It is hard to measure with the eye the scope of this retreat.

Everybody and everything is dragged into the new course: lawgiver and litterateur, court and militia, newspaper and schoolroom. When a naive and honest Communist youth makes bold to write in his paper: "You

would do better to occupy yourself with solving the problem of how woman can get out of the clutches of the
family," he receives in answer a couple of good smacks
and — is silent. The ABCs of communism are declared
a "leftist excess." The stupid and stale prejudices of un-
cultured philistines are resurrected in the name of a new
morale. And what is happening in daily life in all the
nooks and corners of this measureless country? The press
reflects only in a faint degree the depth of the Thermidorean reaction in the sphere of the family.

Since the noble passion of evangelism grows with the
growth of sin, the seventh commandment is acquiring
great popularity in the ruling stratum. The Soviet moral-
ists have only to change the phraseology slightly. A cam-
paign is opened against too frequent and easy divorces.
The creative thought of the lawgivers had already in-
vented such a "socialistic" measure as the taking of money
payment upon registration of divorces, and increasing
it when divorces were repeated. Not for nothing we re-
marked above that the resurrection of the family goes
hand in hand with the increase of the educative role of the
ruble. A tax indubitably makes registration difficult for
those for whom it is difficult to pay. For the upper circles,
the payment, we may hope, will not offer any difficulty.
Moreover, people possessing nice apartments, automobiles,
and other good things arrange their personal affairs without unnecessary publicity and consequently without registration. It is only on the bottom of society that prostitution has a heavy and humiliating character. On the heights
of the Soviet society, where power is combined with comfort, prostitution takes the elegant form of small mutual
services, and even assumes the aspect of the "socialist
family." We have already heard from Sosnovsky[14] about
the importance of the "automobile-harem factor" in the
degeneration of the ruling stratum.

The lyric, academic, and other "friends of the Soviet
Union" have eyes in order to see nothing. The marriage
and family laws established by the October Revolution,
once the object of its legitimate pride, are being made
over and mutilated by vast borrowings from the law
treasuries of the bourgeois countries. And as though on

purpose to stamp treachery with ridicule, the same ar-
guments which were earlier advanced in favor of unconditional freedom of divorce and abortion — "the liberation of
women," "defense of the rights of personality," "protection
of motherhood" — are repeated now in favor of their limi-
tation and complete prohibition.

The retreat not only assumes forms of disgusting hypocrisy, but also is going infinitely farther than iron
economic necessity demands. To the objective causes pro-
ducing this return to such bourgeois forms as the payment
of alimony, there is added the social interest of the ruling
stratum in the deepening of bourgeois law. The most
compelling motive of the present cult of the family is
undoubtedly the need of the bureaucracy for a stable
hierarchy of relations, and for the disciplining of youth
by means of forty million points of support for authority
and power.

While the hope still lived of concentrating the education
of the new generations in the hands of the state, the
government was not only unconcerned about supporting
the authority of the "elders," and in particular of the mother and father, but on the contrary tried its best to separate
the children from the family, in order thus to protect them
from the traditions of a stagnant mode of life. Only a little
while ago, in the course of the first five-year plan, the
schools and the Communist Youth were using children
for the exposure, shaming, and in general "reeducating"
of their drunken fathers or religious mothers — with what
success is another question. At any rate, this method
meant a shaking of parental authority to its very foundations. In this not unimportant sphere too, a sharp
turn has now been made. Along with the seventh, the
fifth commandment is also fully restored to its rights —
as yet, to be sure, without any references to God. But
the French schools also get along without this supplement, and that does not prevent them from successfully
inculcating conservatism and routine.

Concern for the authority of the older generation, by
the way, has already led to a change of policy in the matter of religion. The denial of God, his assistance, and
his miracles was the sharpest wedge of all those which

the revolutionary power drove between children and parents. Outstripping the development of culture, serious propaganda, and scientific education, the struggle with the churches, under the leadership of people of the type of Yaroslavsky,[15] often degenerated into buffoonery and mischief. The storming of heaven, like the storming of the family, is now brought to a stop. The bureaucracy, concerned about their reputation for respectability, have ordered the young "godless" to surrender their fighting armor and sit down to their books. In relation to religion, there is gradually being established a regime of ironical neutrality. But that is only the first stage. It would not be difficult to predict the second and third, if the course of events depended only upon those in authority.

The hypocrisy of prevailing opinion develops everywhere and always as the square, or cube, of the social contradictions. Such approximately is the historic law of ideology translated into the language of mathematics. Socialism, if it is worthy of the name, means human relations without greed, friendship without envy and intrigue, love without base calculation. The official doctrine declares these ideal norms already realized — and with more insistence the louder the reality protests against such declarations. "On a basis of real equality between men and women," says, for example, the new program of the Communist Youth, adopted in April 1936, "a new family is coming into being, the flourishing of which will be a concern of the Soviet state."

An official commentary supplements the program: "Our youth in the choice of a life-friend — wife or husband — know only one motive, one impulse: love. The bourgeois marriage of pecuniary convenience does not exist for our growing generation" (*Pravda*, April 4, 1936). So far as concerns the rank-and-file working man and woman, this is more or less true. But "marriage for money" is comparatively little known also to the workers of capitalist countries. Things are quite different in the middle and upper strata. New social groupings automatically place their stamp upon personal relations. The vices which power and money create in sex relations are flourishing as luxuriously in the ranks of the Soviet bureaucracy

as though it had set itself the goal of outdoing in this
respect the Western bourgeoisie.

In complete contradiction to the just quoted assertion
of *Pravda,* "marriage of convenience," as the Soviet press
itself in moments of accidental or unavoidable frankness
confesses, is now fully resurrected. Qualifications, wages,
employment, number of chevrons on the military uniform,
are acquiring more and more significance, for with them
are bound up questions of shoes, and fur coats, and apartments, and bathrooms and — the ultimate dream — automobiles. The mere struggle for a room unites and divorces
no small number of couples every year in Moscow. The
question of relatives has acquired exceptional significance.
It is useful to have as a father-in-law a military commander or an influential Communist, as a mother-in-law
the sister of a high dignitary. Can we wonder at this?
Could it be otherwise?

One of the very dramatic chapters in the great book
of the Soviets will be the tale of the disintegration and
breaking up of those Soviet families where the husband
as a party member, trade unionist, military commander,
or administrator, grew and developed and acquired new
tastes in life, and the wife, crushed by the family, remained
on the old level. The road of the two generations of the
Soviet bureaucracy is sown thick with the tragedies of
wives rejected and left behind. The same phenomenon
is now to be observed in the new generation. The greatest
of all crudities and cruelties are to be met perhaps in the
very heights of the bureaucracy, where a very large percentage are parvenus of little culture, who consider that
everything is permitted to them. Archives and memoirs
will someday expose downright crimes in relation to wives,
and to women in general, on the part of those evangelists
of family morals and the compulsory "joys of motherhood" who are, owing to their position, immune from
prosecution.

No, the Soviet woman is not yet free. Complete equality before the law has so far given infinitely more to the
women of the upper strata, representatives of bureaucratic, technical, pedagogical, and, in general, intellectual
work, than to the working women and yet more the peas-

ant women. So long as society is incapable of taking upon itself the material concern for the family, the mother can successfully fulfill a social function only on condition that she has in her service a white slave: nurse, servant, cook, etc. Out of the forty million families which constitute the population of the Soviet Union, 5 percent, or maybe 10, build their "hearthstone" directly or indirectly upon the labor of domestic slaves. An accurate census of Soviet servants would have as much significance for the socialistic appraisal of the position of women in the Soviet Union as the whole Soviet law code, no matter how progressive it might be. But for this very reason the Soviet statistics hide servants under the name of "working woman" or "and others"!

The situation of the mother of the family, who is an esteemed Communist, has a cook, a telephone for giving orders to the stores, an automobile for errands, etc., has little in common with the situation of the working woman, who is compelled to run to the shops, prepare dinner herself, and carry her children on foot from the kindergarten — if, indeed, a kindergarten is available. No socialist labels can conceal this social contrast, which is no less striking than the contrast between the bourgeois lady and the proletarian woman in any country of the West.

The genuinely socialist family, from which society will remove the daily vexation of unbearable and humiliating cares, will have no need of any regimentation, and the very idea of laws about abortion and divorce will sound no better within its walls than the recollection of houses of prostitution or human sacrifices. The October legislation took a bold step in the direction of such a family. Economic and cultural backwardness has produced a cruel reaction. The Thermidorean legislation is beating a retreat to the bourgeois models, covering its retreat with false speeches about the sacredness of the "new" family. On this question, too, socialist bankruptcy covers itself with hypocritical respectability.

There are sincere observers who are, especially upon the question of children, shaken by the contrast here between high principles and ugly reality. The mere fact of the furious criminal measures that have been adopted against homeless children is enough to suggest that the socialist legislation in defense of women and children is nothing but crass hypocrisy. There are observers of an opposite kind who are deceived by the broadness and magnanimity of those ideas that have been dressed up in the form of laws and administrative institutions. When they see destitute mothers, prostitutes, and homeless children, these optimists tell themselves that a further growth of material wealth will gradually fill the socialist laws with flesh and blood.

It is not easy to decide which of these two modes of approach is more mistaken and more harmful. Only people stricken with historical blindness can fail to see the broadness and boldness of the social plan, the significance of the first stages of its development and the immense possiblities opened by it. But on the other hand, it is impossible not to be indignant at the passive and essentially indifferent optimism of those who shut their eyes to the growth of social contradictions, and comfort themselves with gazing into a future, the key to which they respectfully propose to leave in the hands of the bureaucracy. As though the equality of rights of women and men were not already converted into an equality of deprivation of rights by that same bureaucracy! And as though in some book of wisdom it were firmly promised that the Soviet bureaucracy will not introduce a new oppression in place of liberty.

How man enslaved woman, how the exploiter subjected them both, how the toilers have attempted at the price of blood to free themselves from slavery and have only exchanged one chain for another — history tells us much about all this. In essence, it tells us nothing else. But how in reality to free the child, the woman, and the human being? For that we have as yet no reliable models. All past historical experience, wholly negative, demands of the toilers at least and first of all an implacable distrust of all privileged and uncontrolled guardians.

NOTES

1. Figures vary on the amount of child-care facilities available in the Soviet Union. One source, ("Women in Russia," by Susan Jacoby, April 4 and 11, 1970, *New Republic*), a woman who lived in Moscow and claimed her figure was given in Moscow newspapers, says day care is available to only 25 percent of preschool children. Another reference, taken from *Soviet News,* London, February 10, 1970, "Report of the USSR Central Statistical Board of Fulfillment of the 1969 USSR Economic Development Plan," says that day care is available for 70 percent of urban preschool children and a smaller percentage for rural children.

2. Party propagandist is a translation of the Russian word *agitator*. A creation of the October Revolution, the *agitator* is someone whose job it is to explain the party's program and policies to the masses. They maintained offices in all parts of the country and conducted street lectures, as well as working in every office, shop, and school. The conference referred to here was just one of the numerous conferences these party propagandists held.

3. Komsomols are the Communist Youth leagues.

4. N. A. Semashko (1874-1949), an Old Bolshevik, who was People's Commissar of Public Health in 1923.

5. Shaturka is an affectionate term for Shatura.

6. "Smychka" was Lenin's word for the "fusion" or alliance between workers and peasants that was the basis of the Soviet state.

7. These are references to the attempts by the capitalist countries and the counterrevolutionary forces within Russia (the White Guard) to overthrow the revolution. Clemenceau and Churchill were leading advocates for intervention on the part of France and Great Britain respectively. Kolchak was a czarist admiral who, after the Soviet power had been temporarily overthrown in Siberia, came there as a puppet supported by the Allies. In November 1918 the Cossack chieftains elected him supreme commander. When the counterrevolution suffered defeat, he was left stranded by the Allies and was arrested and executed. Denikin was also a czarist general who became one of the leaders of the counterrevolution. After Denikin's defeat, Wrangel, a "more liberal" general, was elected by the White Guard as commander-in-chief. He succeeded in remaining in the Crimea for almost a year, but in the fall of 1920 his forces were liquidated, and he was compelled to flee.

8. Bonapartism is a Marxist term describing a dictatorship or a regime with certain features of a dictatorship during a period when class rule is not secure; it is based on the military, police, and state bureaucracy rather than on the parliamentary parties or a mass movement.

9. Leonid Krassin (1870-1926), an Old Bolshevik, People's Commissar for Foreign Trade from 1922 to 1924.

10. "Thermidor" was the month, according to the new calendar proclaimed by the French bourgeois revolution, in which the radical Jacobins led by Robespierre were overthrown by a reactionary wing within the revolution that did not go so far, however, as to restore the feudal regime. Trotsky used the term as a historical analogy to designate the seizure of power by the conservative Stalinist bureaucracy within the framework of nationalized property relations. Since capitalist property relations were not restored, Trotsky advocated *unconditional* defense of the workers' states against the imperialist governments, while he called at the same time for a *political* revolution to throw out the Stalin bureaucracy, whose ruinous policies strengthened the danger of capitalist restoration.

11. The three years following the revolution were a period of civil war in which the economic life of the country was totally geared to the needs of the war. "Military communism" was

adopted to systematically regiment consumption, with top priority going to military purposes. This led to increasing conflict between the workers and the peasants as industrial production declined drastically and grain was requisitioned and confiscated from the peasants. To revive the economy, in 1921 the New Economic Policy (NEP) was adopted as a temporary measure allowing a limited revival of free trade inside the Soviet Union and foreign concessions alongside the nationalized and state-controlled sections of the economy.

The first five-year plan for economic development, which was begun in 1928, projected a modest acceleration of industrial growth and an irresolute policy toward the individual peasant. Suddenly the bureaucracy reversed its position and called for fulfilling the five-year plan in four years. The resultant speed-up and forced collectivization of the peasantry led to a period of economic chaos and great hardship for the population.

12. The Stakhanovist movement was a special system of speed-up in production introduced in the Soviet Union in 1935, which led to great wage disparities and widespread discontent among the masses of workers.

13. Louis Fischer (1896-1970), an American, was a European correspondent for the *Nation* whom Trotsky accused of sympathies with Stalinism during the Moscow trials.

14. Lev Semyanovich Sosnovsky (1886-1937) was one of the early leaders of the Left Opposition, and one of the last inside the Soviet Union to capitulate to the Stalinist faction. Earlier in *The Revolution Betrayed,* Trotsky referred to "the well-known Soviet journalist, Sosnovsky, [who] pointed out the special role played by the 'automobile-harem factor' in forming the morals of the Soviet bureaucracy. . . . The old articles of Sosnovsky . . . were sprinkled with unforgettable episodes from the life of the new ruling stratum, plainly showing to what vast degree the conquerors have assimilated the morals of the conquered" (p. 103).

15. Emelian Yaroslavsky (1878-1943) was a leader of "The Society of the Godless," an organization designed to conduct propaganda against religion. He was a member of the Presidium of the Central Control Commission and was coauthor of

the official charges brought against Trotsky by that body in
July 1927. He wrote a textbook in the 1920s falsifying Bolshevik history under Stalin's direction. He was denounced
by Stalin in 1931 for permitting "Trotskyist views to be smug-
gled into" his history, because, while his book extolled Stalinism, it did not glorify Stalin himself.